HOW

TO

WRITE

AND

GET

IT

PUBLISHED

In deference to librarians in particular, the first edition title of *How To Write Everything Better And Get It Published* has been changed to this new title, *How To Write And Get It Published.*

ACKNOWLEDGEMENTS

Many people have been helpful over the years, but the following have been most helpful in giving *How To Write And Get It Published* a good life.

Dauna Coulter
Jean Crone
James Daniels
Frank Fleming
Joel McWhorter
  McWhorter Design, Inc.
Mona Mitchell
Rhett Parrish
  Source-1, Inc.
Jennifer Searle
Johnathon Searle

HOW
TO
WRITE
AND
GET
IT
PUBLISHED

by

David Strode Akens

*

Edorts Publishing Company, Inc.
abookcoup@aol.com
http://www.edorts.com
1 800 655 7240

This Book Is Dedicated To

Anyone With An Unpublished Manuscript
The Anyone Of Course Including C. N.

Library Of Congress Control Number:
2001132209

ISBN 0-87397-996-6

First Printing 1995
Revised And Enlarged 2002

TABLE OF CONTENTS   5

TABLE OF CONTENTS

TABLE OF CONTENTS

FOREWORD

It's been six years since release of *HOW TO WRITE EVERYTHING BETTER AND GET IT PUBLISHED*, first edition. This new edition incorporates readers' suggestions, such as need for more details about selling manuscripts to publishers, or about printing and publishing manuscripts ourselves. An interesting aside has been the tendency of some writers to skip chapters about writing and jump instead to those featuring publishing.

In this edition, the chapters about writing have been condensed, and those about publishing expanded. This condensation of writing chapters has resulted from taking our own advice. After six years of letting the book "cool," we've decided that we could say the same things better in less space. Writing certainly is a learning process. Some savant has compared it to rowing across the North Atlantic in a bathtub. May our pages lessen the waves, if not the wind?

It could be helpful to keep at least one of your manuscripts (if you have one) in mind as you read this or any other book about writing. Try to compare points in your manuscript with points in a book or article about writing.

Most of the time this book's gender is masculine, but only because switching genders seems distracting. And oh yes, as we row and row and row our boat, one other thing. This masterpiece features fiction writing rather than factual because it seems that fiction encompasses factual and not vice versa.

The first set of writing helps that I remember had to do with the "five W's and the H," initially in reference to writing news stories, then to full-length books. It stems from Rudyard Kipling's oft-quoted, "I had six honest serving men, They taught me all I knew, Their names were what and why and when, and how and where and who." This then leads to six basic questions, most of which the author should answer as early as possible in a storyCpreferably in the first couple of pages. Otherwise the disappearing reader.

Who is the story about?
What is the story about?
Why are the characters there?
When is the story taking place?
Where is it taking place?
How is it best told?

Well, it's best told, presumably, after only two more points. First, realize that today's writer must confront and conquer more than traditional turbulent writing seas. Second, note that bathtub or no bathtub, we've come a long way since Kipling.

Printing and publishing are expanding almost exponentially because of electronic technology. Readers have new questions about choosing which firms to do what. Pardon our flippancy, but the answer is "cautiously." I state this after publishing several hundred books for other people and after several decades as a book printer myself.

Recently the mail brought me a Publishers Marketing Association list of printers that someone wants graded. Within the past year or so, I've dealt with almost half the printers on that list, and I shuddered as I began grading. But that exercise inspired this book's detailed information about printers.

So forward we go. There are four terms to remember, no matter who ends up with what: Traditional Printing, Printing On Demand, Electronic Printing, and Audio.

In Traditional Printing, the author releases his manuscript to an editor, agent, publisher, or printer. The manuscript can consist of typed pages (called camera-ready if they are), or more recently an author-generated file or files.

The new Printing On Demand is a printing technique that, by definition, features incremental printing. In Printing On Demand, your manuscript is in the files of some computer guardian who can crank out another copy by pushing a button, or possibly two.

In printing a few hundred copies or less, Printing On Demand normally is cheaper than traditional printing with its more elaborate and thus costly "pre-press" costs. But even so, though probably the cheapest way to go for short runs, the potential for Printing On Demand is startling. Not only is book distribution threatened as we know it through wholesale and retail outlets, but time between author creation and publication really receives its come-uppance. Yes, an author on limited budget can see his masterpiece in print promptly for only a few hundred dollars, if not less, in Printing On Demand.

The magic word in "Printing On Demand" is "Printing." No matter who claims what, the author seeking wide distribution is probably looking for a publisher (featuring sales and distribution as well as printing) rather than a POD with its emphasis just on the latter.

In Electronic Printing, manuscripts do not appear as ink on paper but instead as images on monitors such as computer screens. Electronic Publishing seems destined to dominate the worldwide publishing scene.

Audio publication will also help shape a future unlike anything yet seen or heard as customers, such as travelers, listen to rather than read publications. It appears that, in the future, authors will have to worry not only about how their work comes across on paper, but also about how it sounds, smells, and, on the positive side, even how it tastes.

TRUISMS IT IS BETTER TO HAVE KNOWN AND BETTER STILL TO KNOW

Thirty-Seven Writing Truisms

1. As long as it stays intact, a paragraph may be of any length; it can be a short, single sentence or a paragraph of many sentences.

2. Limiting each paragraph to a single topic serves as a recognizable guide to the reader. The start of each paragraph is a signpost to him that a new plateau in the story path has been reached.

3. Good writers tend to avoid one-sentence paragraphs, though an exception is made for sentences of transition—and of course for dialogue.

4. We can speak 100,000 words in a good conversational day. Yet most people do not write 100,000 words in a lifetime.

5. The best way to learn to write is to write.

6. The active voice is usually more direct and vigorous than the passive.

POOR

The ball was thrown by me.

BETTER

I threw the ball.

7. Fiction writers write for emotional impact.

8. A good writer puts his ideas in meaningful order and works up to a compelling climax.

9. A good writer manipulates word sequence for emphasis.

10. As a rule, begin each paragraph with a sentence that suggests the topic or with a sentence that helps the transition.

11. Good writers recognize cliches and avoid them.

12. Breaking long paragraphs in two, even if not necessary for meaning or logical development, is permissible if it helps visually.

13. More than 500,000 words are listed in the biggest dictionaries. Of course, no writer comes close to mastering them all. Writers select words that interest them, and that they believe will communicate most effectively with readers.

14. Some writers are intrigued by locations and situations that they themselves enjoy; others by people and things they find distasteful.

15. When a sentence is shortened, it often becomes stronger. Brevity can be the soul of good writing.

16. Fish for single words to replace double words:

POOR

not honest
did not remember
did not have much confidence in

BETTER

dishonest
forgot
distrusted

17. The two chief resources at a writer's command are his imagination and his observation.

18. Avoid using unnecessary expressions such as "the fact that."

19. It has been said that after writing a million words, an individual abruptly knows that he or she is a writer.

20. A writer must keep together the words that are related in thought and keep apart those that are not related:

POOR

She missed her train at the station which was late.

BETTER

At the station she missed her train, which was late.

21. Normally the subject of a sentence and the principal verb should not be separated by a phrase or clause that can be transferred to the beginning:

POOR

The pitcher, in the fifth inning, pitched a good game.

The fighters, without doubt, are very brave.

BETTER

In the fifth inning the pitcher pitched a good game.

Without doubt the fighters are very brave.

22. Most good writers keep a notebook.

23. Put the emphatic word or words of a sentence at the end.

24. The other prominent position in the sentence is the beginning. Any part of the sentence other than the subject is emphatic when placed first:

> The art of forgiveness he had never learned.

> Fat and lazy, never one to exercise, he nonetheless makes a good living at wrestling.

> Fifteen is the number.

25. There are half a million words in our language, but *ten* of them comprise twenty-five percent of all written and spoken English. These are the ten: a, and, I, in, is, it, of, that, the, to.

26. Only fifty words encompass *half* of all written English.

27. To receive special emphasis, the subject of a sentence must take the position of the predicate:

> Riding across the desert came a solitary figure.

28. The principle that the end is the prominent position applies equally to the ending of a sentence, to the sentences of a paragraph, and to the paragraphs of a piece of writing.

29. Of all the parts of speech, perhaps none can be more confusing and yet more significant than the verb. For instance:

> A woman tiptoes across a porch.

She strides across the porch.

She swaggers across the porch.

She stumbles across the porch.

She strolls across the porch.

30. Statisticians report that *ten* prepositions account for more than ninety-five percent of all prepositions used in writing. These frequent prepositions are: at, by, for, from, in, like, of, on, to, with.

31. The easiest way to remember the part of speech known as *conjunction* is to separate it as conjunction and imagine it as a connective.

32. The parts of speech are important to a writer because they generally are considered to rank in order of importance. The first choice for expressing an idea is a verb, the second is a noun, and the third is an adjective or an adverb. The remaining four parts of speech are simply grammatical helpers used to support the main parts of speech. For example, suppose that the idea of traveling thrills you. You might try to express this in the following ways:

I *love* to travel. (The verb expresses your idea)

My *desire* is to be a traveler. (Perhaps a noun approach)

I am a *dedicated* traveler. (Or perhaps an adjective)

It is not difficult to sense that the verb version of the preceding sentences is the most meaningful expression of the idea (in addition to the fact that the verb *love* in its own right is a strong word); the noun *desire* in the second sentence is more general and so has less impact. And the adjective *dedicated* sounds general and pat.

33. We should remember this basic rule: give preference to the verb rather than the noun, and to the noun rather than the adjective or adverb.

34. Simplest of all verb forms is the infinitive consisting of the preposition *to* followed by the verb. Such as: *to run, to walk, to write.* A *split infinitive*, scowled upon by many writing purists, has one or more words between the preposition and the verb, such as: *to partly fill, to properly use, to slowly walk.* Normally, it is better not to split an infinitive.

35. Writing talent can't be taught. These things can be taught: how to look for story ideas; how to choose subjects that sell in today's market; how to best organize a story.

36. Writing is not so difficult—or at least not that difficult. If a person can talk, he can write. The would-be author simply knows something and wants to share it with someone else. Writing simply makes what one has to say more permanent.

37. A writer must first try to please himself. Thoughts of fame and fortune should be secondary. When he has finished his story, he should be able to say that this is his best work; this is his statement. Only with this can he really feel good about it.

CANDIDATES FOR WORDS MOST OFTEN MISUSED IN THE ENGLISH LANGUAGE

ABOVE. Let's not use **above** if we can avoid it, if the meaning is preceding:

NO

The **above** names are...

The **above** is an example.

YES

Simply use **these** or **this**.

These facts illustrate.

This is true of the preceding paragraph.

AGGRAVATE, IRRITATE. Aggravate means to add gravity to a situation that is already bad. We avoid using it to mean **irritate.**

NO

We **aggravated** the driver behind us.

YES

An accident **aggravated** the traffic situation ahead of us, causing us to **irritate** the driver behind us.

ALREADY, ALL READY. Already means previously, or by this time. **All ready** means that everything is ready.

NO

It is **all ready** time for a break.

YES

We are **all ready** for a break.

It is **already** time for a break.

AMOUNT, NUMBER. Amount suggests bulk or heaps of things; **number** suggests amounts that can be counted.

NO

There was a large **amount** of rocks and a larger **number** of coal.

YES

There was a large **number** of rocks and a large **amount** of coal.

AND/OR. We avoid this clause unless we really must use it; it's an aggravating rail switch.

NO

I feel strongly toward those and/or others.

YES

I feel strongly toward those **and** others.

AWHILE, A WHILE. We use **a while** only when we desire to emphasize a period of time. Usually we're looking for the single word **awhile:** linger awhile; his talk lasted **awhile** longer.

NO

The tyranny lasted for **a while**, and we suffered **a while** longer.

YES

The tyranny lasted for **a while**, and we suffered **awhile** longer.

BAD, BADLY. If we feel **badly**, something is wrong with our sense of touch; if we feel **bad**, we're miserable. Remember: **bad** rhymes with sad.

NO

My bones ached, causing me to feel **badly**.

YES

My bones ached, causing me to feel **bad as** I felt badly for my elusive glasses on the floor.

CAN, MAY. Can means "is able to;" **may** means "has permission to."

NO

Can I take sick leave today so that I **may** take some medicine?

YES

May I take sick leave today so that I **can** take some medicine?

CONTINUAL, CONTINUOUS. Continual means repeatedly; **continuous** means constantly.

NO

The breeze flows **continually** past the marina, but fishermen **continuously** fish regardless.

YES

The breeze flows **continuously** past the marina, but fishermen **continually** fish regardless.

DISINTERESTED, UNINTERESTED. Disinterested means impartial, without a selfish interest in the matter. Attorneys search for **disinterested** judges and jurors for their clients. At the same time they try to avoid those who seem **uninterested.**

NO

He yawned because he was **disinterested** in the **uninterested** jury's verdict.

YES

He yawned because he was **uninterested** in the **disinterested** jury's verdict.

DUE TO, BECAUSE OF. Begin a sentence with **because** of, such as **because of** circumstances, conditions, or otherwise—not with **due to**.

NO

Due to the condition of the field, we could not play.

YES

Because of the condition of the field, we could not play.

EVERYDAY, EVERY DAY. We wear our **everyday** clothes **every day**.

NO

She wears her **every day** dress **everyday** to class.

YES

She wears her **everyday** dress **every day** to class.

EVERYONE, EVERYBODY. Both of these are singular; avoid the common mistake of using "their" with them.

NO

Everybody has their own price.

YES

Everyone has his own price.

Everybody has his own price.

FIRSTLY, SECONDLY, THIRDLY. These are archaic. Instead we use "first, second, third" and so on.

NO

Thirdly, I'd like to point out…

YES

Third, I'd like to point out…

HANGED, HUNG. People are **hanged;** pictures are **hung.**

NO

The vigilantes **hung** their victim, and they later **hanged** a picture featuring the event.

YES

The vigilantes **hanged** their victim, and they later **hung** a picture featuring the event.

HEALTHY, HEALTHFUL. A person can be **healthy,** but an apple can be **healthful.**

NO

He felt **healthful** after eating a **healthy** apple.

YES

He felt **healthy** after eating a **healthful** apple.

LIKE, AS. Too many writers make the mistake of using **like** when they mean **as.** Our ears can help us with this one; unless our hearing tells us otherwise, we can go with the majority of good writers and favor **as** over **like.**

NO

We spent the afternoon **like** we did last summer.

The water looks good, **like** lake water should.

There is no fool **as** an old fool.

YES

We spent the afternoon **as** we did last summer.

The water looks good, **as** lake water should.

There's no fool **like** an old fool.

THAT, WHICH. Let's apply a rule of thumb that is almost foolproof. We use **that** if the group of words it introduces is *not* set off by commas (This is the house **that** Jack built, **which** incidentally or not so incidentally still isn't paid for).

NO

The town, **that** is marked on the map, is my home town **which** I really love.

YES

The town **that** is marked on the map is my home town, **which** I really love.

SUBJECT

Reading Some And Writing Some

Read Better To Write Better

Select the genre (category) in which you most enjoy reading, read widely in it, and then write in it.

Definition Of A Good Story

One or more characters solve one or more problems.

Unfamiliar Stories

In creating a story an author should look for one that is unfamiliar. A good author should also be a good reader. Among other things this should help the author avoid a story that the editor or other readers fault as "old hat," a frequent reason for rejection.

The Classic Theme In A Story

The classic theme (subject) in a story is good versus evil.

Three Ways To Imagine A Story

1. Start with a setting that interests you.

2. Or start with a character who interests you.

3. Or start with an incident that interests you.

Originality

Beginning writers should avoid experimenting. If you want to express originality, let your characters do it for you.

Reading Time Versus Writing Time

Balance your literary time between reading and writing. Certainly we can't sell thousands of copies merely by reading. But in the long run we probably can't sell thousands of copies without diligent reading.

Too Eager To Write To Read

A creative writing instructor quit his position midway through his career. His reason: "I'm tired of dealing with students so eager to be recognized they won't read." So he began teaching a course in reading. "But my readers kept asking me how to write."

But Reading What?

Let's say that we schedule fifty percent of our literary time to reading and fifty percent to writing. Of the fifty percent allocated to reading, let's give maybe twenty-five percent reading time to our favorite genre and twenty-five percent to professional literature about writing and marketing. A writer should fight the urge to write more and read less, unless he's "on a roll" with a particular manuscript.

Underlining

Here's another thought about reading about writing. Underling might help. At least before books skyrocketed in price, it seemed wise to purchase books and underline them for future reference. It probably still is.

Six Types Of Fiction

The main categories of genre fiction are mysteries, romance, westerns, historical, science fiction, and adventure. They average from 55,000 to 85,000 words--short compared to many mainline novels.

Reading And Writing In The Category You Like

Again, writers should be avid readers. First, the writer should read widely until he selects the genre he most enjoys--the genre he should concentrate on. Then the writer should read voraciously in the category selected, in particular the most recent releases. The first time around he might well read for pleasure and the second time around hopefully for profit. Janet Dailey, one of the top romance authors, reportedly read 400 Harlequins before attempting to write her first one. Her reading time was worth it. Today Dailey's books in print are in the millions.

Obtaining Publisher Guidelines

If your reading suggests a publisher who is publishing books you like best, you could send him an SASE (self-addressed stamped envelope) and request guidelines in the category of interest. If you receive such guidelines, treasure them. A manuscript that obviously does not fit a publisher's preferences most likely needs to go elsewhere.

Writing Can Be Learned

A major lesson learned in time is that *you can learn to write.* It may take a while, but eventually you can. As goes the axiom, "Genius is one percent inspiration and ninety-nine percent perspiration."

Many Talented Authors Find Learning Difficult

Authors with genius talent in some writing areas tend to have problems improving in other areas. So, many talented writers find it difficult to be published in today's highly competitive writing market. Most assuredly there are boxes, and sacks, and lockers, and trunks, and dresser drawers out there crammed with yellow notebooks or typed manuscripts prepared by people with outstanding talent. They surely have not yet learned the rules for improvement. Any venture calls for guidelines, and writing calls for more guidelines than most ventures. Even Lewis and Clark needed a map. Real writers, of whatever talent, should be willing to apply that ninety-nine percent perspiration. Something about life calls for improvement with time. Many things matter not, but it does matter and matters greatly how we play the game. With our boots off or on, on board or overboard.

Learning Writing Techniques By Reading Other Authors

In reading to improve writing (compared to reading for pleasure the first time around) the reader-writer can learn by second-guessing the method used by authors in obtaining writing effects. Does the viewpoint change? Should there have been dialogue instead of narration?

Selecting A Subject

Select a subject that attracts you and that you believe will attract readers as well. Is it a subject you are enthusiastic about? Then decide if a story about that subject fits a need no one else has met. And is it a need you can meet better than others?

Reading More And Writing More

Undoubtedly, most people will agree that it is much easier to publish better than to write better. For ninety-nine percent of us, becoming a better writer means lonely vigils in a cabin of dedication while outside on various decks merry passengers and perhaps even crewmen party galore. Much reading and revising must occur—not rest and relaxation. A grasp of the wheel through weather fair and foul.

Publishing is more fun than writing. We enjoy friendly and exciting company. Each year in the U. S., more than five thousand new publishers publish, (a number increasing rapidly), with four-fifths still afloat the following year. There can be smooth sailing also if an established publishing conglomerate takes us on. But, even so, we remain vigilant. For one thing, our publishing date with major publishers is almost always at least a year or two downstream. And, even so, we often find ourselves swept aside by one or more bestsellers capturing our publisher's dynamics (spelled promotion budget), while we sail blinded by salt spray from a distant sea, the tear-causing kind.

But Writing Or Publishing How?

In addition to publication by others, there is a new self-publishing tide, thanks in part to modern technology with words such as Printing On Demand (POD) and E-publishing (Electronic Publishing). Self-publishing is easy, especially now. We see a local printer, or even self-styled photo copier, or more recently a so-called online or electronic printer or publisher (the latter presumably helps sell books). He or she in turn flashes someone else's publication as a model. We hand over our key-boarded (if not voice-generated) copy, sized similarly to a page from a model publication, throw in a cover we've had someone letter similar to one we like, and stand back. Within days or even hours we have completed the printing of a book.

Of course, the selling of our book is something more, as we'll find in the following pages. But since right now the fun part of our trip is just beginning, let's celebrate as we travel to success. We're selecting our trip, so let's also select enjoyment. After publishing our book, we don't need to tell anyone exactly what's sold, do we? A sign on our cabin wall can read, "Admittedly, after publishing somewhat less than a million copies, we at that do have more than one copy left." So maybe we're not in this as a business, after all. Yet we should be, shouldn't we? Many pleasing answers climax later on.

So—shall we say—with sales unfurled—onward!

THINGS TO LOOK FOR IN SETTINGS

How Real Is Your Story's Setting?

Can you visualize your setting so distinctly it is real to you? Would it help to base your setting in a place in the real world you actually know?

A Story Should Not Conflict With Its Setting

Don't use an exotic setting (the Amazon jungle or Shangri-La) for a story that might as well have taken place in Road Junction, Colorado.

Each Setting Has Its Own Characteristic

In your setting try to note buildings or businesses or parks, for example, different from those in Houston or Springfield or New York. What kind of music? What kind of newspapers or magazines? Are the people friendly or unfriendly. Do they banter or are they sinister?

A General Impression Followed By A Few Significant Details Is A Frequent Winner In Describing Settings

You can't expect to describe any setting completely. One proven approach is to first give a strong general impression, as general as this statement: "The stream seemed to flow inexorably toward endless time and space." Then add a few pertinent details, for example: "The water, swirling against increasingly large boulders, gurgled angrily in transit." Or for the morbid, "The room had the sweet odor of a recent funeral." Then icing to the cake: "A surviving flower petal hid on the floor as if crunched by the wheel of a casket carrier." If you have a general impression followed by a few significant details, almost all readers can fill in the rest.

Be Consistent And Timely When Mentioning Directions In A Story

If you plan to use such descriptions as north, south, east, or west, be sure to establish their correct usage from the start. If your heroine has escaped down a mine shaft in order to race in and out of crawl spaces, then the reader should be reminded at this point that this is the western mountain. The reader may have envisioned the heroine escaping into the eastern mountain and turning left, and so we're interfering with the reader's right to visualize the scene.

Author Needs To Know Setting In Detail

Very seldom will you need to describe details of a setting, but you yourself do need to know the setting, including details. The author should know the location of the halls, closets, stairs, telephones, baths, garage, sidewalks, fences, fireplaces, air conditioning units, television connections, washing machine, dryer, den, recreation room, master and smaller bedrooms, kitchen, and dining room. You don't want your characters running into each other in slippery, uncarpeted hallways.

Author Should View Setting Through A Wide Lens

The author must know what is outside the house as well as inside. Is the street well-kept or ill-kept? The neighborhood? The author must know the outside also in order to know the characters. For example, your local stockbroker will not be canvassing in the Bowery, unless perhaps he took his own financial advice.

You Have The Freedom Of A Creator In Your Own Fictional World

It is your story and your characters, and you alone have the right of eminent domain in whatever world you choose to create. If you desire for your characters to commandeer a school, you may have them do so en toto. If you want to clear a school of teachers and students, but leave the school buildings and playground exactly as you remember them in real life, you may do so. If you want to clear a space for your fictional characters to meet during half-time of the Super Bowl, you may do that too. You may prefer to wipe a whole county or even country off the map and replace it with one of your own as Faulkner did with Yoknapatawpha County and as Tolstoy did essentially with Russia. You may prefer to mix the factual and the fictional fifty-fifty, surrounding your cleared fictional space with real places and people.

Modern Authors Minimize Preliminaries To Scenes Or Chapters

In former years story-tellers often began a scene or a chapter with a detailed description of the setting followed by an introduction to the scene to follow. Today such description and introduction tend more and more to be minimized, either absorbed into the scene or chapter itself or given short shrift in some other way.

Us And Them Setting

Some successful authors think of setting in terms of "us and them." For example: Tennessee Valley Authority damming the Tennessee River and bringing electricity and recreation to isolated communities and individuals as in the book, *Wild River,* the ageless jokes about the slick city traveler asking directions of the country bumpkin.

Unforgettable Settings

Some of the world's most popular stories have unforgettable settings: *War And Peace, Alice In Wonderland, The Adventures Of Sherlock Holmes, Gone With The Wind, The Great Gatsby, Last Of The Mohicans, Tom Sawyer, Uncle Tom's Cabin, David Copperfield, Elmer Gantry,* and *Main Street.* Lucky is the author who can make a particular setting his own bully pulpit. Unlucky is he if the setting he's selected is already taken. An intriguing setting can further a subject's longevity immeasurably.

Real Neighbors Can Help Authenticate Fictional Settings

Some authors prefer to use real communities, streets, hotels, and the like in their scenes, such places adding authenticity to their fictional setting. Your setting, whether city or town or river or wherever, can and often should relate to factual objects nearby. The names of known places in its area can make the setting much more real. From personal experience a fictional swamp on the northern shores of Choctawhatchee Bay in Florida is even more real because of the swamp's real neighbors—the nearby actual towns of Freeport and Niceville and Valparaiso and Highway 331. References to these actual locations help give authenticity to a fictional swamp.

CREATING CHARACTERS

"Entering Deeper Literary Waters"

Leading Character Most Important

Make the leading character far more important than any other character.

Create Fictional Characters Who Remind Readers Of Real People

The first thing book editors or publishers as well as readers look for is integrity of characterization. Unless the author has an innate ability to write characterization, and do so with facility, he would be well-advised to stick to real characters. At least, prior to writing his first novel he should study one or two "main" characters from real life and use them closely in forming his main characters. As he does this, though, he should remember that close does not mean identical. For example, one way to avoid exactness is to change the person's sex and age. Thus we retain closeness without duplication. What better springboard toward creating fictional characters who seem real? Eventually these characters take on lives of their own. They no longer will be identifiable as people in real life, against which we disclaim in the front of our work, "either living or dead."

Look at picture books or television sets or movie screens for your characters' faces, especially pictures in color. Or base your characters loosely on people you know or have known. As an author sees an interesting face, an interesting character starts to form in his mind. Create characters whose actions and dialogue remind readers of people in real life reacting under similar circumstances.

Protagonist Equals Antagonist

In the best stories the protagonist and antagonist are evenly matched and equally motivated. The protagonist is working hard to solve his problem, and the antagonist is working just as hard to keep him from it.

Let's Give Our Major Characters A First Drive

Start by giving our characters, certainly our major characters, a strong first drive: greed, ambition, love, obedience, hate, vengefulness, courage, fear, asceticism, and the like. Stories portraying characters with these traits are proven winners. With human nature comes a desire to find a central mission in life, and it is a relief to find someone who believes he possesses it. With that person leading the way, we can make it through the flames. We realize instinctively that the driven character's unusual behavior is certain to get him in trouble eventually, but he will fight hard to overcome. It is in tune with our own survival instinct and sense of immortality.

Then Let's Give Our Major Characters A Second Drive

To be really developed, our major characters need a second as well as a first drive, and these drives need be in conflict with each other. Hamlet's first drive was to talk instead of act, to put off decision-making. His second drive was a desire for revenge against his father's killer, a drive that clashed head-on with his indecisive nature.

In a novel entitled **Wild River,** inhabitants of the Tennessee Valley loved their beautiful valley with its Tennessee River. Such love was the first drive. Then came the overpowering Tennessee Valley Authority, whose dam caused water to engulf cabins and understandably created strong reactions in valley residents. They determined to resist the dam, resistance translating into their second drive. The German spy, in a World War II novel **Eye Of The Needle,** had as his first drive loyalty to Nazi Germany. His second drive was his attraction for a housewife who saved his life and ministered to him.

Then there is the classic story of Abraham and Isaac. Abraham was one hundred and Sarah ninety when God answered their prayers and gave them a son Isaac. Talk about love for a son. Love—what a drive! Then God orders the very religious Abraham to sacrifice his son. So Abraham now has his second drive—Godly obedience. Can we really imagine the internal conflict, the plot ramifications within a father when God orders him to destroy his beloved son? This scenario is played out centuries later in the New Testament account of God sending his son Jesus as a sacrifice. First drive versus second drive—the hallmark of good characterization within a protagonist.

Two drives in a major character are much more meaningful than one. If someone has a drive to walk on high wires, it isn't that big a deal. But if a second drive is fear of heights, it is. If someone desires to be a public speaker, then join the crowd. But what if the second drive is timidity in general and stage fright in particular? If so, we have the basis for a suspenseful, riveting plot.

Your Protagonist Really Needs To Worry About His Second Drive In Particular

Each protagonist needs to recognize the danger presented by his second drive. If your protagonist proceeds blithely to take the second drive in stride, as if confident he can handle it, then the reader may blithely close the book. Many stories begin successfully with a protagonist who is capable and colorful and otherwise interesting and who seems capable of solving the problem of the second drive. But then this protagonist moves along too self-assuredly. He is too confident of solving his second-drive problem. After all, he is the protagonist, so he knows as the author knows that he will win in the end. He acts as if he knows he can handle anything. The confident protagonist doesn't worry; in fact he has little doubt that in the end he triumphs and all will live happily ever after.

Well, the reader is not happy, starting with the moment the protagonist is cocksure instead of recognizing the second drive as a big problem with an uncertain outcome. In mediocre fiction there too often is a hero who doesn't worry. But the protagonist of a skilled writer is troubled greatly by the second drive. Who is going to worry about the second drive if the protagonist doesn't? Not a former reader.

Your Victim In A Mystery Needs Enemies

If he headed a Scout troop and then volunteered for the Peace Corp, you had better discard him. If, however, your victim invented the guillotine or could have, then your sleuth will be blessed by many strong motives.

A Series Character

Authors should consider the advantages of creating a series character. For one thing, what could be more real to you, and hence the reader, than a character or characters you shepherd through a number of books?

Main Character

Your main character should be at least as real to you as are some of your friends. And as with those friends, this principal character should be sympathetic, so much so that the reader wants to pull for him. He doesn't have to be perfect—far from it—but definitely worth pulling for.

Interesting Religious Characters

Surprisingly, popular religious characters depicted by twentieth century authors, other than a few exceptions, are rare.

Reader Empathy With Characters

Readers should like and admire one or more main characters, such characters of course including first-person narrators. These are the folks with whom a reader would like to spend several hundred pages.

Remember, the characters we create will be our role models; we may want to avoid characters too reprehensible for us to play their part, to occupy that character's mind and body at least during the time we write our story. Maybe we'd rather not play Attila the

Hun. Perhaps we don't want to play the role of Jack the Ripper or Lizzie Borden throughout the writing of our manuscript. Maybe we'd prefer the role of Othello or Mona Lisa. There's another advantage to being an author: as an author we can be both director and character. It's our play and our cast. If we select characters that we find likable and intriguing, the chances are that our reader will find them likable and intriguing too. The choice is ours.

Create Characters Who Are Not Stereotypes

In creating your characters, don't forget originality and variety. One step in creating original characters is to avoid stereotypes. Examples of character models that have been overused to the point of stereotyping are Sherlock Holmes's sidekick Watson, the dumb blond a la Marilyn Monroe, the no-holds-barred cops like Mike Hammer and Lew Archer, and the coquettish Southern female as with Scarlett on verandas and in garden swings. Instead we should try to make our characters different. If we can make them do the unexpected and yet be believable, we're arriving. Can we create a believable cab driver who suffers from motion sickness; a President Truman whose favorite island retreat is Japan; a politician who's an introvert; an Ollie North who manufactures lie detectors? If not, at least we can set our sights a la different.

It is all right to give both your major and minor characters a stereotypical profession, but do not make your characters stereotype members of that profession. You can have your university professor sit in a tower shrouded with ivy, but don't encumber him with a pipe and manuscripts and shelves of dusty tomes. Instead, let him surprise you with his collection of sports photographs, his souvenir from Algiers, and his tapes of rock-and-roll or country music. He can be a scientist or an inventor, but instead of being mad have him fondling a $100,000 check from Uncle Sam for a research project, or have him eyeing a plaque awarded him by the Spaceless Paranormal Society For Mind Over Matter.

Again, resist the impulse to stereotype your characters, in particular as related to their occupations. The reader can do that himself. Why should he pay good money to have you do it? Maybe your pilot is afraid of heights. Or your general is a peace-loving man. Listen to what your inner self is saying about them as you communicate with their inner selves; find out what they want and plan to do. At least some will improve your plot for you.

Variety Among Characters

As for variety among our characters, we shouldn't make them all bright or all dumb, all rich or all poor, all Episcopalians or all snake handlers. If one character is lascivious, another could be a Trappist monk. Madame Bovary was adventuresome and over-hormoned. Her husband was stodgy and circumspect. She wanted lovers in divers places; he was not at home on the high diving board.

Some Authors Create The Inner Lives Of Their Characters Before Creating Their Physical Appearance

If your tendency is toward introspection and intuition, "inner lives first" may be your best bet. Only after the inner lives of your characters come alive to you will you turn to their outside appearance. You first define your characters' psychological makeup as the reason for their behavior. Our genes, our ancestors, our upbringing, our background—heredity and environment—still affect our inner selves as they do our physical appearances. So, to understand a character we must understand the character's past as well as his present. The characteristics list in this section offers words for character identification. Only after you feel that your characters actually exist somewhere can you set about giving them identifiable physical characteristics.

Some Authors Learn Their Characters By Seeing How They React To A Problem

Instead of first writing background information concerning a character, some authors begin by deciding how a character would react to a serious problem. For example, your protagonist is in a party boat that explodes about a mile offshore, sending its passengers into shark-infested waters. Would your protagonist even consider for a moment striking out alone toward shore and safety? Instead, would he not instinctively look for someone to try and save? But what if among his victims is a beautiful girl and an old man who reminds him of his grandfather perhaps. Or a teenage cheer leader versus another teenage female, this second one resembling leftovers at a football banquet. Is there something about the protagonist or the protagonist's background that would affect his decision? Once an author who uses this approach decides how his characters would react in an unusual situation, it should be clearer how the character will react in any situation.

A Character Portrait Sketch

A characterization technique that can be effective is for you, the author, to draw rough sketches of your characters and hang them in front of your typewriter or computer throughout the writing of your story. The sketches can help implant the characters in your mind and make them less difficult to describe in your story.

Too Many Characters

Unless you are writing a "family saga," or otherwise using a wide canvas, avoid the confusion of having too many characters. Instead, where possible, combine the functions of two characters into one.

Create Characters Who Contrast Sharply

For your most dramatic stories, look for characters who contrast sharply with each other. Give your reader a character to love and a character to hate.

Things To Avoid In Naming Characters

When selecting your characters' names, avoid similar sounds and using the same first letter. Be wary of names difficult to pronounce, and avoid in particular difficult names that sound similar.

Characters Make Your Story

Your most memorable stories are the ones with the strongest characters. Through the creation of strong characters with strong motivations and conflicts, the story begins to grip the reader. Strategic placing of scenes in your story gives it vitality and moves the storyline forward, but your characters illuminate these scenes.

A Character Need Not Be Admirable To Earn A Reader's Sympathy

Reader sympathy can depend upon a character's situation. The reader sympathizes because a character suffers, then struggles against the suffering as the reader would like to do in a similar case. The reader wants to cheer a fighter because he considers himself one. A character does not have to be admirable to elicit a reader's sympathy, though positive characteristics will help. The man whose wife was killed by an assailant might be a mobster. He might even have wasted someone else's spouse. But if the mobster suffers from his wife's death, the reader will sympathize with him; and if the mobster determines to find his wife's murderer, the reader will pull for him likewise.

Authors Know Characters As "Real" People

In great novels people have apparent lives of their own, beyond the end of the book, and this is because these characters are real to the author. It can be assumed that they mean more to the author than does his book.

Offering An Impression Of Your Character

Each of Tolstoy's characters is a center of vision. Each of them looks out on a world that is not like the world of the rest, and we know it. So wrote Percy Lubbock: "Tolstoy expresses the nature of all their experience; he reveals the dull weight of it in one man's life or its vibrating interest in another's; he shows how for one it stirs and opens, with troubling enlargement, how for another it remains blank and inert. He can create a character in so few words—he can make the manner of a man's or a woman's thoughts so quickly intelligible." Great novelists have the power of offering an impression of what they know. "Tolstoy knew he could make a living creature of Anna by bringing her into view in half a dozen scenes. But he needed to set the stage for her."

Character Traits Identified

To assist in creating major characters, some authors identify their major character trait or basic drive on a 3 X 5 card. Then they spread the cards on a table, and let the characters start to materialize from these words.

A Sympathetic Villain

The modern villain, with all his faults, has some aspect of character that makes him vaguely sympathetic, perhaps even likable. Some reference to the oft-quoted abused background, though not an excuse, can create sympathy.

Most Villains Have Contempt For Law And Lawmen

Villains are breaking the law and to this point getting away with it. A classic reason for a villain's contempt for the law and law abiders is that the villain considers the latter stupid or dishonest or both.

A Protagonist That The Reader Would Like To Be

The easiest and usually best way to make your reader live in your story—which is where you want your reader—is to give the reader a protagonist he himself would like to be. In a happy-ending story, the reader assumes the protagonist's role.

The Conflicts Inside Your Protagonist Drive Your Story Forward

The conflict between the first and second drives inside your protagonist causes exterior conflicts that propel your story forward. The conflict in a story should stem from the conflicts in the mind of your protagonist. Physical action is not necessarily conflict, but internally your protagonist's first drive versus second drive is.

Your Protagonist Will Contain Quite A Bit Of You

In addition to being a combination of people you know, your protagonist will contain quite a bit of your own personality. Writing instructors are continually advising beginning writers to write about people and places they know. Professional writers have already learned this from experience. A writer can write effectively only about people experienced firsthand.

Among Other Faults, Your Antagonist Is Conceited

Your antagonist believes that he is the hero of your story. The antagonist may be a society, for example, not necessarily a character. If it is a society — perhaps in science fiction — the society itself feels that it is the hero of the story, overwhelming and perhaps squelching individual characters if not other worlds.

The classic, Robin Hood, has survived in printed form and continues to spawn various movie and television versions. Robin Hood's inner conflict involves conformity versus justice. His belief in justice results in his becoming an outlaw. Instead of climbing a mountain, he is hounded in Sherwood Forest. His interior struggles surface through the action of the unscrupulous Sheriff of Nottingham, perhaps representing the devil himself. Conflicting with Robin Hood's sense of fairness is the sheriff's despotism, and so Robin and the sheriff are enemies. The writer will remember that though the protagonist Robin Hood has a first and second drive, other characters need only one. In antagonist Nottingham's case his drive, with staying power, is conformity to the law as he interprets it.

In Robin Hood, as with any story classic, various kinds and degrees of struggle occur. There is Robin's inner struggle to see justice done, and the sheriff's to maintain law and order. Robin struggles to help the poor. In addition, externally he is dodging arrows in the forest, sometimes even jousting with his own men, typically for fun. His highest mountain, in fact, is a footlog from which Little John has a devilish amount of fun upsetting his hero opponent. Robin and various other outlaws have fights, again perhaps in the spirit of devilish fun. Meanwhile, the sheriff, in addition to chasing Robin, chases the even larger goal of supporting Prince John. Prince John is the cunning brother of Robin's monarch choice, King Richard the Lion Heart. There are conflicts galore, as there should be in any classic.

WRITING CHARACTER BIOGRAPHIES

A good first step in writing character biographies is to fill in a form similar to the following for each character. The form will provide ready points of reference during biographical preparation and development.

CHARACTER CHARACTERISTICS LIST

Can Use Percentages: Such As 60% Serene

A NAME: FIRST, MIDDLE, LAST

AGE:

ATHLETIC: PHYSICALLY STRONG, SKILLFUL, MUSCULAR

ATTRACTIVE: DEGREE OF PHYSICAL ATTRACTIVENESS

BIRTH DATE: MONTH, DAY, YEAR

BIRTHPLACE: TOWN OR COUNTY, STATE

BROTHERS: NAMES AND AGES

EYES: COLOR

FINANCIAL: FINANCIAL ASSETS AND SOURCE OF INCOME

FIRSTBORN: OLDEST CHILD

GOALS: BASIC DRIVE AND OTHER GOALS

HAIR: COLOR

HEALTH:

HEIGHT: FEET AND INCHES

HIGH SCHOOL: WHERE AND WHEN GRADUATED

HOBBIES:

INTELLECTUAL: HOW INTELLECTUAL?

INTELLIGENCE: HIGH INTELLIGENCE; BRIGHT, CLEVER, WISE

LITERATE: EXHIBITS EXTENSIVE LEARNING OR CULTURE

MARITAL STATUS: HAPPILY SO?

OCCUPATION: HOW MAJORITY OF TIME IS SPENT

PARENTS: ATTITUDE TOWARD CHARACTER

PARENTS: PHYSICAL APPEARANCE AND SOCIAL STATUS

RELATIVES: NEAREST RELATIVES, THEIR AGE AND RELATIONSHIP TO CHARACTER

RELIGIOUS: EXTENT OF DEDICATION

SENSE OF HUMOR: DEGREE

SISTERS: NAMES AND AGES

SKILLFUL: EXPERT; AREAS OF ACCOMPLISHMENT

TALENTED: AREAS OF TALENT

TRAITS: NAME BEST TRAITS

TRAITS: NAME WORST TRAITS

WEIGHT: POUNDS

Character Biography Basics

With most authors, character biographies are helpful in developing a story. If you are in this group, you'll write biographical sketches ten to fifty pages long before beginning the story. You need biographies of all your characters, and you need to spell out their relationship to each other. As a guidepost to keep in mind throughout your story, first for starters write a one-sentence description of each character. Then complete biographies of all your characters before starting to write your story. An approach used by some authors is to start their project by jotting down brief character sketches on cards.

The biographical histories of each character can include as few or as many points as desired from the character characteristics lists. As the author uses external tools such as the lists, he should also try to "psyche" his characters by trying to think as they do.

Write a description of the characters as seen through the eyes of another character. This description will enable you to see your characters better by presenting them as seen from at least two perspectives. In addition, it will help you develop the habit of viewing each character as a distinct personality instead of a shadow in the scene. No matter how bizarre or otherwise unusual your character's basic drive may be, you can make it seem reasonable for him if you can show that to *him* it is worth the effort.

A failure in many biographical sketches is lack of detail *throughout* the character's life. Where did he attend kindergarten? What other schools did he attend?

What is the first important event that he remembers? Name some of his most pleasant experiences, and name his most unpleasant. What is unlikable about him and what is likable? What does he think of the other characters? What do they think of him? Perhaps only one percent of what you know about your characters will be detailed in your story. But *you* know the other ninety-nine percent, and your writing will show it without narrating it.

Some authors feel that you don't need to know your characters intimately before you start telling your story. These authors believe that characters will reveal their personalities in their actions. Other authors believe that first they should write a one or two page synopsis of what the story will be about, then a synopsis about twice as long as the first, and only then write character biographical sketches. It is true that the author's story will help his characters become more real to him. The author can't predict how his characters will develop, whether they will play larger or lesser roles in his story. But no matter how accomplished, most professional authors prefer detailed and otherwise intimate character biographies before the writing of a story begins. Again, the book itself won't include nearly all the details from biographical sketches; otherwise the characters would exist only for the story's sake. They wouldn't guide the story, but instead the story would attempt unsuccessfully to guide them.

The author should analyze his characters as if he were a psychiatrist, with his characters fully covered by medical insurance. After writing a biography of ten to fifty pages about each of the major characters, the author should rely primarily on the character characteristics list for his minor characters. Throughout the writing of his manuscript, he should keep this list nearby to help identify both his major and minor characters.

Character Motivation

Many successful stories have parental influence as a primary reason for a protagonist's motivation. Typically the protagonist follows or rebels against the influence of at least one parent.

Characters Need Inner Conflicts

If a character experiences strong inner conflicts, such as a desire for revenge that collides with a feeling of pity, or conscience with lust, only then can a reader experience deep empathy with that character. If characters have no inner conflicts, then the story is a melodrama. Here's an example of a character with inner conflicts:

He felt compelled to kill his mother's new husband to avenge his father's death, yet he was opposed to killing and otherwise was a moral person. In addition he had doubts that his stepfather was guilty, though his father's ghost told him that his stepfather was the murderer. The character, of course, was Hamlet.

Believe In Your Characters

You must believe in your characters and feel deeply about them. If you don't, your readers won't either.

Authors Who Wait Until Characters Come Alive In Their Mind

Many writers who use a character-biography approach will not start writing their manuscript until characters come alive in their mind. To reach this stage, some authors have written biographical sketches not only for each major character but also for all characters in the story, perhaps dividing this description into physical and psychological traits.

Authors Who Emphasize Character Biographies

A number of successful authors spend more time writing dossiers about each character than they do in all other preparation. Fascinating characters can't be developed in depth without the author taking time to do so. The characters must be given time to grow. In the process of developing characters by writing dossiers about them, the authors learn precisely how each character thinks and feels about all the other characters. Authors who find themselves too busy to do this kind of spade work, too often find themselves with characters who are too shallow to carry the story successfully.

An Example Of Opening Paragraphs In A Sample Character Biography

As for the ten-to-fifty page biographies about major characters, many authors write them in first person. Here are opening paragraphs from one such biographical sketch:

"I was born 39 years ago as Otto Keller. I was born to middle-class parents in a middle-class neighborhood in a small town outside a large German city. As I was growing up in Germany, so was Adolph Hitler (physically) and elsewhere Joseph Stalin and Minnie Pearl, and a little later John F. Kennedy and

Robert Kennedy and Martin Luther King and George Wallace in the United States.

"I guess you could say that as a child I was just your typical kid next door. I'm not now nor have I ever been tall and dark and handsome, but that's only because I'm Nordic--I'm blond. As the saying goes, if I were modest, I'd be perfect. I was born with only an average IQ (118 according to elementary school scores) and I made only average grades in that elementary school. I knew my IQ because my forthright mother told me it was only average. But that was before--entirely by accident--an older neighbor introduced me to jugular-grabbing chess. I did not then know, but learned quickly, that mental exercise is the same as exercising body muscles--which I enjoyed doing also--and the more one studies or does crossword puzzles or reads books or plays chess--the more intelligent one becomes. My latest IQ rating is 135--perhaps not genius, but almost. And I plan to play more chess. Other than lack of modesty, I have only one other major bad habit--I break peoples' necks.

"My father was not a neck-breaker, but I never doubted that he had the capacity. Nor did his opponents in semi-pro boxing, or those drunks from his rathskeller that he bounced onto concrete outside the back door like rubber Welcome Mats kicked upside down. My father and mother and my close girlfriend were all killed simultaneously in an Allied air raid on Bremen in 1944. My most notorious neck-breaking is being reserved for Americans.

"But inside me--deep notwithstanding--surely must be that spark of humanity or goodness that many topnotch thinkers credit to every human. In fact, my habit of breaking necks has been a late-bloomer. While growing up I did not like the idea of hurting anyone or anything, including hunting animals. True, as a child I was initiated into a few local hunting forays, but alone with a deer in a forest I found I could not kill it.

"I was hearing about Adolph Hitler before I entered the University of Berlin School of Physics, and even then I wondered why someone didn't assassinate him. The black American author who wrote an article, translated into German, wondering why some black didn't assassinate or at least try to assassinate the leading U. S. racists, such as later Alabama governor George Wallace, or even why whites didn't assassinate leading integrationists such as later John F. Kennedy, Robert Kennedy, and Martin Luther King--well it all made me wonder if it was a less-than-subtle suggestion that someone in Germany should try to readjust Adolph Hitler's skeleton makeup. So that's where I'm now coming from. That in fact is the message in my story: Does association lead to a better understanding, not only of the other person but of the other person's point of view. In other words is it better to suggest, for example, 'Let us reason together,' or to drop an A bomb? Is it appropriate to smell the roses along the way, or to work on the neck of someone like Hitler, for example, so that he ends up walking like a tripod along that same way?"

Many Character Biographies Are Much Shorter And Simpler Than The Preceding Example

All character biographies need not be as involved nor as macabre as the preceding, of course. Modern romances in which John chases Mary, Mary runs, and John catches Mary—or vice versa—may involve less than complex characters and often do.

Making Characters Believable

A major help in making characters believable is to emphasize the basic drives that motivate them, again such as love, hate, greed, and fear. The character's jealously, his hunger for recognition and power, are believable drives that will help make the characters believable. What caused a character to develop his particular drives to start with? His past should help explain it.

A Character's Profession

A character's profession is an important guide to understanding him. When you can't change the character's occupation without substantially changing character and plot development, then be reassured that you have the correct profession.

One Way To Start Character Biographies

Write down the names of your characters together with a few words highlighting their physical or mental characteristics. Then write one-sentence descriptions of your major characters' goals or desires.

Character Development

A character without flaws has nowhere to grow. Further, a character with flaws is more believable.

What Kinds Of Problems Would Hurt Your Major Characters Most?

To strengthen your major character's first drive, bring aboard a second drive that would hurt the first drive most.

Your Readers Must Sense That At Least Your Major Characters Had And Have A Life Before Your Story Starts And After It Ends

This does not mean several paragraphs of exposition before your story starts or after it ends, almost always a fatal flaw at the start and often at the end. But the fact that your main characters arrive with a basic drive should suggest their past, and their handling of that drive at the end should suggest their future.

Your Characters Should Fascinate You

Luckily, if you find your characters fascinating, it is more likely your readers will find them fascinating.

Character Conflict Creates High Drama

Insistence versus resistance is the basis of conflict in characterization. When characters have different goals and insist on achieving them, conflict erupts. If the stakes are great, and both sides prove unyielding, the result is high drama.

Life And Death Situation

An ideal way to increase substantially a story's interest is to have a character find himself in the same life-and-death situation from beginning to end—for example, a war story in which at any point a soldier may be killed. Similarly you can use a kidnapping. Or the danger may be less obvious: a character may have a terminal illness, and throughout the story the reader will wonder if the character will outlive the story. Of course, life-and-death situations mean different things to different people. It is not necessary that the hero of every story almost drown or otherwise face death. To some, the respect of peers is as important as life. Many war stories portray peer respect as the basis for courage. Readers read novels in order to share emotions experienced by the characters.

Character Conflict

A basic rule of character stardom is: involve the reader with a character and involve the character with conflict. True reader identification—identification in which the reader forgets himself and becomes involved in the author's world—can only occur with a character who is struggling.

Characters must not only change as the result of hardships they meet, they must struggle if the story is to be dramatic. A reader may sympathize with a character's plight, but true reader identification only occurs with a character who is struggling.

Troubled People

Stories are about people, and people are interesting only when they experience problems and try to overcome them. (Sad but true.) The goal of good fiction is to create a special kind of world. Not a humdrum life, but a life of problem solving, as life is. When the main character is anxious or greatly concerned for a good reason, the reader is anxious and concerned, resulting in the steady turning of pages.

The degree of reward or punishment facing a character in any situation determines the degree of reader interest in that situation. What bounty awaits the character if he succeeds? What terrible catastrophe awaits him if he fails? An anxious protagonist, if he has sufficient reason to be anxious, will generate reader anxiety. Anxiety causes suspense and means that your readers stay with you.

Character Changes

If new character traits come to light as the story flows toward the end, you probably have added a commendable dimension to your story. Your heroine finally comes to the realization that there is room at the top. The Southern sheriff realizes that he should be less cruel, and the reader applauds as he releases the big-city drifter from his chain gang. The villain in the black suit and hat spares his victim's life at the last moment. In a good story, the characters change as the result of the story's events.

Villain Determines Cast

Your villain's shenanigans determine the cast of characters in your story. These characters include those who know or knew the victim, plus those who will right the wrong.

Reader Always Present

Your story's reader, though unseen, is as present as the characters themselves.

Rely On Few Points To Introduce Characters

Don't try to describe your characters so completely that a police artist could duplicate their portraits; let the reader fill in the gaps. Many readers look forward to visualizing the characters in their own way. A suggestion or two about each character at his first appearance or soon after is sufficient: male or female, short or tall, fat or thin, blond or brunette. Don't save any of these descriptions for subsequent pages; if belatedly you describe a character as short, whereas the reader has been visualizing him as tall, your story at least from that point is no longer spell-binding.

Normally in story telling it is better to introduce your character gradually rather than, let's say, drop him in full blast. This is because your reader can identify with your character much more easily if he can meet him in the way one normally meets people in the real world: a little at a time. The everyday satisfaction of gradual discovery is exemplified by expressions such as, "She wears well."

Let Your Character's Personality Emerge A Little At A Time

It is more effective to have your character's personality emerge as the result of character action or reaction in a scene. You can introduce your character as a braggart, if you prefer, and do so with a line of dialogue. But we don't need to know at the start how he became one. Your story will likely be much more effective if you tend to avoid character summaries. Instead, show physical movement or dialogue.

Character Description

One help in revealing a character is to have another character—rather than the author—describe him. Instead of saying, "Sally is intelligent," you can have a character say, "Sally always knows best." Another help in portraying character is, of course, to view a situation through the character's viewpoint. "He had never knowingly hurt anyone. How could they accuse him of being a killer? Now less than an hour to live. Every tick of the clock placed him nearer eternity. Cold and dark and damp. Now came the sound of hollow footsteps. The feel of a rifle's cold nozzle against his perspiring head. Only to end as a hamburger."

Character Believability

If characters are to be at least as believable as human beings, their behavior cannot be predicted accurately most of the time.

Recognizable Characters

The best authors seem to use what might be called "sponge-like" imaginations. They utilize characters that are recognizable and familiar, so much so that readers easily can extend their lives in any direction even beyond the author's words. At the end of the book no major character has ended where he or she expected to end, but the reader knows the characters' futures because of the author's good directions and the characters' pattern of following them.

Main Characters Must Change

Main characters must change in some way. If imprisoned, they can mellow. If wealthy, they can learn to pay the price for those stepped on.

Minor Characters

Make minor characters distinctive and colorful. Poorly revealed minor characters can weaken a story substantially. A chain is only as strong as its weakest link. To accomplish proper characterization of minor characters, more description may be called for. Though some minor characters may have a tendency to steal the show, their author should keep in mind that by remaining two dimensional they permit three dimensional main characters to stand in relief.

Be leery of too much time lapse between appearances of minor characters. And if they're too easily forgettable, don't hesitate to eliminate them.

Characters Without Flaws

If the author has shown a character without flaws, then he has not shown that character through the eyes of the other characters.

Reader Empathy With Characters

When readers like and admire the author's main characters, or dislike and wish for them a deserved punishment, they're with them to the end. Readers like and admire strong people—characters with courage. They like characters who keep trying, who won't let failures keep them down. They struggle, they persist, they go down struggling, and they bounce up to try again. At least women readers (and most readers are women) like strong heroines as well as strong heroes and, surprisingly perhaps, they tend to prefer those with a sense of humor. Readers seem to prefer characters who remind them of people in the real world that they would like to have as friends and neighbors.

Heroines

Heroines need not be pretty, and even pretty heroines often regard themselves as plain. A beautiful heroine will do only if she is sufficiently captivating to overcome this stigma. An overly confident beauty queen can easily find herself alone in the court.

The most durable heroines have in them a certain something that suggests vulnerability. They are brave but vulnerable, and the readers must sense this. A heroine must be susceptible to an easy touch because of her consideration for others, and because her starting position is not from strength but from the weakness of her situation. Still, she triumphs by the time the story ends. She has overcome her problem triumphantly.

Heroes

Webster defines a hero as, "A man of great strength and courage." Though there are other definitions, an author can't go wrong with this one.

Many notable modern heroes are older than the heroine and give evidence of having experienced a surfeit of living. This type of seasoned hero seems to fascinate many modern readers, perhaps women especially. He, in turn, still has left a basic need that only a special kind of woman can fill. Indeed lucky is that heroine who is needed by such a hero. This hero's applause and love are both worth gaining, but of course he should not be considered an easy mark. The hero is not readily susceptible to feminine charms. He remains strong and experienced to the end, master of his own fate as well as the heroine's. This hero must be an active force throughout the story. If he isn't actively present, we must at least be thinking about him.

Add To Your Character Sketches As You Write Your Story

Whether you keep your sketches on 3 X 5 cards, notebooks, or computer files, be sure and add to them as you write your story or otherwise think more about your characters. You don't want your heroine's old flame to pop up in chapter three and then have you forget his name by chapter seven. Jot down every new idea that comes to mind about a character—and that means everything. Again, many of the details will not appear in the story. But the author must know his world creation if it is to be real.

SPECIAL CHARACTERIZATION IN CATEGORY STORIES

A Clever Villain

You want your villain to be as clever as you can make him, and thus a worthy antagonist. The better mysteries have intelligent villains.

Private Eyes More Sophisticated

The methods of many historic private eyes were about as crude as the culprit's he was chasing, but the trend now is toward a more sophisticated protagonist.

Today he is literate and appreciates music and art. He dresses well but casually and has exemplary manners. Often he is a college graduate. Typically he is intuitive, and in fact this protagonist's skills can be of an intuitive rather than analytical nature. In addition to having hunches about characters and events, he will try to reinforce such feelings with solid facts. Hardly ever is he promiscuous.

Today's protagonist in a mystery story usually has a deep sense of family, which translates into a custodial role toward his associates.

Private Eye Receives More Violence Than He Gives

Modern private eyes have a potential for violence, but typically violence is done to them. Private eye James Garner in the "Rockford Files" television series is most often used as a punching bag before getting his man.

Female Private Eyes Carry Weapons

Modern female private-eyes carry licensed guns that they use as a last resort. The trend is toward use of weapons with the same dispatch as their male counterparts.

Modern Mystery Protagonists Are Careful Chroniclers

Modern protagonists are careful chroniclers, whether describing characters, moods, or scenes.

Murderer's Motives

Your sleuth, a keen student of human nature, understands the human frailties that prompt people to murder and knows that the mother of all murders is self interest. Whatever the murderer's motives, whether revenge, sexual drive, greed, or something else, the murderer will consider his motive a necessity as much as a desire.

In A Murder Mystery The Murderer Usually Studies His Potential Victim Closely

In the mystery novel the murderer usually plans his mayhem with deliberation; murder is seldom a spontaneous act. The murderer studies the victim's habits and strikes accordingly. Interesting complications occur when something happens that alters the victim's routine.

Detective Attributes

Often it is effective to bring out characteristics your detective did not know he had: courage, intelligence, resourcefulness, and an intense anger that is aroused because of the injustice of the situation. These character traits develop in proportion to the resistance that faces him and are especially pronounced when loved ones are in danger.

Characters React To The News Of A Murder

Our observant sleuth will carefully note how characters react to the news of a murder.

In Romance Fiction, Humorous Repartee Between The Heroine And Hero Can Add Zest To The Story

The author should not make the humor slapstick or otherwise force it. But sophisticated repartee between the heroine and hero can suggest an ever-closer relationship developing between them. The characters need not necessarily realize that their conversation is funny. But the reader realizes that such repartee suggests their deepening involvement with each other, making their dialogue doubly interesting.

PLANNING YOUR PLOT

Know Your Ending Before You Start A Novel

Consider every ending possible, however unlikely, and select the one that is inevitable. The whole thrust of the story is to reach that goal.

A Basic Plot Formula For Novels

Here is the formula: boy meets girl, boy falls for girl, boy fears he will lose girl, boy eventually wins girl, or he loses her. If you substitute the words "fame" or "fortune" or "wisdom" for "girl," you have covered the basic plot for novels.

Four Ways To Plot

1. Borrow from some traditional plots, such as a plot used in a classic or a current success that the author likes.

2. Base the plot on an actual historical or current sequence of events that interests you.

3. Decide on an initial situation, and plot forward from this situation.

4. Start at the end, with the climactic scene in mind, and work back to the start of your story.

Viewpoint

Selecting the proper viewpoint is simply a matter of deciding who can tell your story best. There are three basic choices: *objective viewpoint, first-person viewpoint,* and *omniscient viewpoint.* In the first viewpoint, the objective, the author does not have access to the mind of any character; but in each of the last two viewpoints, the author has access to the mind of at least one character.

In the *objective viewpoint* the author describes the actions of the characters as if for example the author were describing the scene to a blind person seated beside him at a television set. Here's an illustration:

Mary hurried to the class, and she looked harassed. Her students were really unruly as she entered the room. A spitball barely missed her.

The above is called objective because the author is outside the character, looking at the character objectively, with no idea whatsoever about the characters' subjective state. For this reason authors rarely use the objective viewpoint. Some writers do use it successfully, at times with some detective novels and spy thrillers when the authors desire to create and the readers agree to sit still for characters with an air of mystery but little intimacy. One way to achieve more intimacy with a character in the objective viewpoint is to make guesses about what is going on in his mind. For example: "Maybe she was distraught over the closing of the plant. She certainly acted distraught." The author is not presuming to know what is happening in the character's mind; he only conjectures.

In the *first-person viewpoint* the author has access to one person, the narrator of the story, who is also a character in the story. Here is an example: "I decided to write a book, so I sat on a park bench and observed people passing by. Though I know I looked lazy, I was alert. I could barely wait for someone who looked like a heroine." Most beginning writers choose to write in the first-person viewpoint. But as the author writes his novel, he will find that it takes a surprising amount of skill to handle a long story from one viewpoint. It often is awkward to try to go places where the narrator couldn't have been and show things the narrator couldn't have seen. There also is the potential of boring the reader with the continuous use of "I". In general, the first-person viewpoint seems to be falling out of favor compared, for example, to the omniscient viewpoint. An author preparing to write a novel would do well to consider bypassing the use of the first-person viewpoint.

If the author reveals what is going on in all the characters' minds, the author is using the *omniscient viewpoint.* This viewpoint was popular in the Victorian novels. For example: "John wondered if he felt as bad as he looked. Mary, on the other hand, was happy. She felt like going to the ball. Meanwhile, the coachman felt uncertain. He wondered if he should dust two cushions or one." But because of the constantly changing viewpoint, the reader was not privy to any character's mind long enough to establish reader identification with that character. That is why very few novels today are written in traditional omniscient but instead are written in a restricted version of the omniscient. This restricted version of an omniscient viewpoint is a powerful tool indeed. In this restricted version the author claims access to the minds of only certain characters and not others. These selected characters, normally the protagonist and two or three others, are known as "viewpoint characters." With this approach the author does not ask the reader to change viewpoint too often and yet gives the reader the opportunity to feel intimate with more than a single character.

Whatever viewpoint you use, try to stay in that character's viewpoint at least throughout the length of a scene.

Resolving Minor Plot Before Resolving Major Plot

Most authors resolve the minor plot in their stories before resolving the major one. This helps to keep the main story clear and the ending clearcut.

The "Tree Approach" To Plotting

Across the centuries authors have experimented with ways to plot, one such way entitled a "tree approach." With this approach the author thinks in terms of running the protagonist up a tree (Yes!). Something caused the protagonist to leap into the tree, and whatever caused him to do this probably is the start of the story. A bear perhaps? Rising floodwaters? Mobsters in pursuit? A need to scout enemy territory? Would-be kidnappers? The discordant roar of an unhappy electorate. A need to make a living as a Hollywood stunt man or woman?

Throughout the body of the story the writer throws rocks at this treed protagonist, and in the concluding portion gets him out of the tree. This it would seem is an unusual though interesting exercise. But at least you can imagine throwing a few stones at your protagonist, to get his attention, and then throwing ever larger ones until you get him from the tree.

The Climax Approach To Plotting

Still another plot approach is to think in terms of a series of climaxes, each climax more intense, each worrying the reader more. The final climax should most certainly be the mother of all climaxes. If a boulder, it is the largest boulder in the stream. If a rock, it is large enough and thrown hard enough to knock our protagonist out of any tree.

Most Successful Stories Involve A Struggle Between A Protagonist And An Antagonist

The protagonist's inner struggle of first drive versus second drive assumes an external role with the arrival of the antagonist (villain). The antagonist attacks the protagonist at the latter's weakest point, namely the first drive. The antagonist thus amplifies the protagonist's inner struggle by giving it this external role. The antagonist should not be mindless evil, a villain who arrives in the black cowboy outfit just because the story needs an adversary. Black-suited villains are too cardboard, and beginning writers in particular should be on guard against using them. The antagonist does not realize that he is the story's villain. He considers himself the hero. No one from Attila the Hun to Hitler and Stalin has considered himself motivated simply by a desire to be cruel and hateful and otherwise sadistic. Human nature is such that a person believes that everything he does—no matter how horrible—is completely justified and maybe even angelic.

The story of Abraham and Isaac is a classic plot, with the devil rounding out the plot as the villain. Consider Abraham's first drive as love and his second as obedience. The devil's idea of love and obedience, of course, conflicts with Abraham's. To the devil, love of self comes first and obedience to self is a necessity. Certainly not to God. So on Abraham's way up the mountain with Isaac it is easy to imagine potential problems. Perhaps the devil in the form of a person or a brigand of enemy warriors appears in the father-and-son's path. Maybe there's a series of fights and maneuvers all the way up the mountain, each an increasing threat to Abraham in his planned ascent.

Conflict in the Abraham story features his inner struggle coupled with his physical struggle to take his son up the mountain. In addition to the inner struggle there are the many physical hindrances to an ascent, problems ranging from enemy warriors to forks in the path to rock slides. And in addition to these apparently never-ending hardships, there is the overriding conflict: the struggle between God and Lucifer for Abraham's soul. Allegiance to God versus allegiance to self.

The Minor Plot Defined

Minor plot is what almost everyone else calls subplot. Except that the English *sub* is the derivative of the Latin words *under, below,* or *secretly* as in submarine or subterranean and thus isn't what a so-called subplot does in literature. So for clarity let's brashly use the terms major plot and minor plot, as in major characters and minor characters. A minor plot comprises a series of relatively minor events that usually relate to the major plot. The minor plot adds momentum to and otherwise embellishes the major plot. One important goal of the minor plot is to furnish stronger revelations about the major characters in the major plot. Here is an example:

Our thirty-nine-year-old heroine Betty Collins works for Insurers International. Her job is to belt insurance scammers as ordered. Meanwhile a couple from Canada is "scamming" the Gulf Coast, filing gross negligence claims against resorts, most often related to slippery diving boards. The couple makes reservation at the White Sands, on Florida's northwest Gulf Coast. Insurers International wants Betty to work undercover as a lifeguard, always in reach of her camera. The major story is apprehending the couple. However, Betty happens to be unusually attractive, and the resort manager's son begins spending so much time in the pool his hair turns green from the chlorine. Betty jokingly addresses him as 'greenie,' but will their relationship extend beyond that? This is the minor plot. Betty never wavers from her determination to nail the Canadian couple. Yet the minor plot shows a softer view of someone who can be, again to coin an expression, hard as a rock.

For best results the minor plot should connect in some manner to the major one. Also, normally the minor plot characters connect in some manner with one or more major plot characters. Moving from the major to the minor plot for short periods of time can add effectively to suspense by giving the reader something else to worry about. Or the minor plot can add comic relief, lightening the mood if the major plot has been so intense that a sprinkling of humor seems advisable.

Setting, Scene, Summary

Remember the three "S's" of plotting a novel: setting, scene, summary. This applies from the opening page onward.

Accelerate Action And Events, And End With A Climactic Chase

Keep increasing and rising conflict foremost in your mind as you plan your novel. Your characters, your protagonist in particular, should face ever more difficult obstacles. The difficulties should continue to increase in number and intensity until finally the climactic scene— often involving a chase.

Outlines

Story outlines, normally written as text rather than indented by numbers, tell you where you have been and where you are going. Before you write your manuscript, outline it, starting with a one-sentence story summary. Most professionals would never start to write their book without preparing an outline. Some of the best plots have developed as their authors prepared an outline. Ken Follett has revealed that he outlines his book repeatedly, with the final outline version perhaps reaching 30,000 words or more. Of course outlines by most authors are much less.

A Well-Plotted Story Is Like A Mountain Stream With Boulders

It may help to consider the plot of a story as a stream with boulders at fairly regular intervals breaking the stream's surface. These are the points of conflict along the length of your story. Let's say that a stream starts from a mountain waterfall. A huge boulder, the crucial situation at the start of your story, is at the base of the waterfall or a very short distance downstream. From the huge boulder a series of smaller boulders increase in size and stature, causing larger eddies as water flows toward a second huge boulder guarding a lake. Secondary conflicts (smaller boulders) may agitate the stream's flow. The second and last huge boulder represents the final great obstacle your protagonist must pass before reaching that great placid lake that we can call nirvana. In the lake the conflicts recede rapidly. If we wish—and since it's our story we can do as we wish—the lake represents the larger than life possibilities projected by a good story. If we have enough "bigger and badder boulders," causing eddies down the stream to the lake, we have the ideal plot structure.

But again, does our suspense mount steadily? In other words, using our stream analogy again, will the boulders down our stream have the same size and hardness as would a string of pearls, or will the boulders be a series, with each becoming larger and harder? Meanwhile, do we remain wary lest any boulder down the stream loom larger and harder than the big one at the climax?

Real streams have haphazard obstacles. Fictional streams have an orderly series of boulders that feature an increase in size and hardness and slipperiness until the final huge barrier and then the placid lake. The reader has an innate craving for order and significance that calls for a pattern and makes fiction a necessity.

WRITING YOUR PLOT

Summarizing Chapters

Write a chapter-by-chapter summary of your story before you start writing your manuscript. The summary can be only a few paragraphs per chapter, or longer if desired.

Sources For Plot Ideas Abound

Many writers have long found newspaper stories to be an ideal source for plots. Books have helped others. But in general, ideas for plots come from everywhere: overheard conversations, weather, dreams, television programs, newspapers, books, vacations, work. The more you hone your writing skills, the more readily will ideas for plots come to mind.

Starting With A One-Sentence Story Summary

Some authors prefer to start their writing project by jotting down a one-sentence summary describing what their story is about. They keep this sentence as a visible reference throughout their writing of the manuscript. It's as easy as the following:

Write a single sentence describing the story you have in mind. If you should need help, start by composing several sentence candidates. Study these and then compress them into that single sentence you wanted, then display this as a reminder to yourself while you write your story. Here is an example of a single sentence intended to describe a story:

This is the story of the struggle between marijuana growers and timbermen.

Now Write A Brief Synopsis Of Your Story

This synopsis can be, say, 500 words or less. Let something happen, even if it's wrong. Doing it takes precedence over accuracy. Try to complete it at one sitting.

Write Chapter Headings And Brief Descriptions

One or two sentences should summarize what happens in each chapter. Each chapter should feature a major event.

An Outline Or A Longer Story Summary?

There are two schools of thought concerning what should happen here: either an outline or a longer story summary. Because both an outline and a story summary are helpful and require relatively little time or effort, why not do both? The outline, of course, should consist of a listing of the major events that will occur in your story. In addition to serving as a handy map showing your story's route, it permits flexibility in the order of your writing, should you desire to visit ahead or back or venture off the beaten path. This longer summary could be, say, around 2,000 words. Even writing this summary three or four times can be increasingly helpful. Rewards from steps such as these offset the cost in time and effort.

Visualizing Scenes Before Plotting

Though most authors plot first, some writers begin their story-writing process by first visualizing one or more key scenes that they believe will have powerful emotional impact. They visualize such a scene as if seeing it on television, and then they write the scene as they see it. If they can feel emotional impact from such a scene, they are reassured that they are on the right track. The order in which the scenes appear is unimportant. Authors can move the scenes around as the story unfolds. For authors who believe in really getting their ducks in a row before starting to write a story, this approach can be combined with the preceding story summaries.

The "What If?" Question

One technique that aids in plotting is known as the "What if?" question. What would happen if the heroine shoots the son of the local police chief? What would happen if the hero sides with her against the chief? What if the chief's son had been the local high school football star? What if the setting is Texas with big-time gambling involved in high school football rivalries? What if the mob surfaces and the hero and heroine find themselves pitted against some not-so-dumb wise guys? "What would happen if?" are four important words that can be very helpful in plotting.

Plotting Suspenseful Scenes

Prolong the suspense as long as you can throughout a scene.

A Writer Can Greatly Improve His Plotting By Studying How Other Writers Plot

For example, it has been said that Leo Tolstoy's power of "making a story tell itself" is unsurpassed. Writers read Tolstoy to learn his techniques.

Protagonist Needs A Problem

In plotting make sure that your protagonist faces a problem, most likely a problem that continues through most or all of your story. It should be a problem that the protagonist can do something about. Readers like for their protagonists, hero or heroine, to solve such problems not by sitting and looking at them but by taking strong action. In every chapter the protagonist must <u>act</u> at least in some measure. Or it must be indicated that the protagonist plans to act. The reader must realize that the protagonist is not simply sitting still; to have the protagonist merely worry about something is not enough.

Readers Crave Justice

Readers crave to see justice triumph. Hamlet's fans desire justice following the murder of his father. Matt Dillon will forever make sure that villains in Dodge City experience an ordeal of fire.

Keep The Plot Simple

A mistake that writers make too often is to complicate the basic plot with clutter. Is our basic plot as simple as possible? We do not want to clutter it with characters and scenes that tend only to confuse it. Who killed John is the main plot. John's widow is attracted to the funeral director. Now there is a major plot and a minor plot. But you don't want the widow also trying out for the Olympic swimming finals, unless the funeral director is one of the judges. In other words, too many plots spoil the landscape.

Some Successful Authors Construct Their Plots By First Envisioning A Protagonist Against An Antagonist

From the beginning the protagonist is strong and sympathetic, and the antagonist is similarly strong. The strength, of course, need not be physical. Highly successful stories have been written against a background of chess games and solving crossword puzzles. They place two strong characters "face to face," in conflict with each other, and let them lead the way in building the plot. The opening requirement for the two combatants is simple. They need something to joust about and a stage on which to do the jousting.

Stories In Which The Protagonist's Life Is Threatened Are Strongest

Of many excellent plots, all proven winners, most successful is the one in which the protagonist is in a fight for his life — literally.

A Story Synopsis

A most important step in plotting a story is to write a synopsis. Sadly, this most important step is too often ignored. Another important step, almost as important, is to keep this with you throughout the writing of your story. If you use a word processor, this means that you should make a file named "synopsis" and file it in the directory named for your story. Without such a synopsis, your story may wander about like a stream out-of-bank. Unless you can plot your way down this stream with a spyglass, you may be navigating blindfolded.

Thankfully, though, writing a synopsis is much easier than controlling a stream out-of-bank. A short description of an item is the basic approach to selling almost anything. With a synopsis as a primary tool, agents and editors and publishers negotiate contracts with or for many professional authors. Although pre-published authors normally must complete their books before receiving contracts, they nonetheless need a synopsis as a sales piece to influence an agent, editor, or publisher.

It is easier to write a synopsis before rather than after you write your story. If you wait till after you write your story, you have to consider the extra scenes that developed as your wrote. But better late than never. If you have an unpublished manuscript and are concerned as to why it isn't selling, then a synopsis can come as near as anything to suggesting the reason. Similarly, you may think of overlooked flaws if you write a description of an object you have to sell.

In writing a plot synopsis, probably the best and easiest start is to write a single sentence describing what your story is about—the theme if you want so to call it. Then write a sentence identifying each of your characters. Next jot down a few dramatic scenes—two to four depending on the length of your story—and for a short while mull over what you've accomplished. Then write your synopsis of a dozen or so pages. Then simply follow your synopsis while writing your story. Your first two or three paragraphs can become chapter one; perhaps your next three paragraphs can be chapter two, and so on. Additional scenes and other additions will develop as you write your plot.

The Ticking Clock Factor In Plotting

The time factor can be an important element in making your plot click. Over the centuries authors have used the "girl tied to the railroad track" scenario to give suspense to their plot. (Before trains it was the girl tied in the path of the impending avalanche or perhaps dinosaur.)

Minor Plots In Relation To Major Plots

Longer stories probably will need one or more subplots (minor) in addition to the main (major) plot. By longer story is meant stories of about 70,000 words or more. As the number of words increase, most authors discover that the plot needs to branch off into one or more smaller branches in order to handle the flow. No matter how many branch streams, however, we should remember that the main stream is the reason for the branches and remains our main concern until the end. Sometimes branches try to become a main stream themselves. Similarly, it is quite easy for some aggressive characters to try to take charge of the story. But minor characters should never be permitted to overshadow the main character or characters. Some branches appear to flow independently of the main stream for long stretches whereas other branches clearly merge with the main stream from time to time.

A *parallel subplot* can be lifted in its entirety from a story without changing the main stream flow. For example, the main story may be a captain's struggle to bring his ship to port during a storm. A parallel subplot could be the attraction between the first mate and a rich and beautiful divorcee on board to play. The captain could be concerned lest the first mate break the rules against fraternization with passengers, but the captain's struggles with the storm remain, with or without the first mate's dallying.

In the *interactive subplot* the captain is so concerned about the first mate's dereliction of duty, he finds it difficult to concentrate on piloting his ship. To remove that aspect of conflict would be to remove an obstacle faced by the captain. The best subplots are the interactive, especially if they arise out of the basic conflict.

A second-level subplot is a relatively small branch that flows from either an interactive or parallel subplot. In the case of the ship captain in the storm, a second-level subplot could involve the captain's heart condition versus his first mate's handling of the pilot wheel or the divorcee. A story can have both interactive and parallel subplots and—again as with a stream—both offshoots can merge with each other or with the major plot course.

Here Are Three Typical Review Questions For Book-Length Stories

(1) What is the point of the story?

(2) Is each scene necessary?

(3) Do the subplots relate to the main story line?

There Is Nothing New In Fiction Plots

There are no new plots. Every fiction plot has been used thousands of times, with all contemporary fiction stories indebted to previous ones. However, though all contemporary fiction relates to previous fiction, good writers add their own unique touches in a fresh and lively manner. The good writer startles and surprises and shocks (more than soothes).

No reader has read all those other plots, nor has any writer. Nonetheless, some readers, not least among them editors, have read enough to make originality a hallmark of good writing.

Chapter Length

Try to maintain a chapter length of no more than ten or twelve pages, and for scholarly works maybe even less. True, some masterpieces contain chapters with more than twice that length. But, for one thing, most of these antedate the influence of television with its more rapid moves from scene to scene. Also, why grab someone by the collar for unnecessarily long periods of time? Release the pressure before the color purple hues. Give those readers a breather between rounds. Also, it is a good idea to try to keep chapter lengths somewhat even. Television aside, it is much more pleasant to ride an even-gaited horse than one that alternates between bucking and trotting. The reader is searching for order in life—at least one small step. If the author wants to vary the pace to help keep the reader awake, then try varying the length of scenes in a chapter. Good writers keep readers firmly in mind.

A Strong Romantic Minor Plot Can Strengthen Most Major Plot Lines

For starters, a romantic minor plot can be a major help in added understanding of those major characters that carry the main story. Readers, male as well as female, are strongly interested in the love lives of the major characters. Not melodramatic or otherwise mushy revelations but a good love story showing emotional motivations. As for sex, adult bookstore buyers aside, most readers prefer reading the emotional involvements related to anticipation rather than to reading about the sex act itself. The revelation of character rather than rote lovemaking is what counts more in today's good storytelling. Finally, with these points in mind, it should be stated that almost all popular novels include a good love story.

Upheaval, Again As With A Boulder In A Stream, Is A Basic Plotting Technique

If you are having difficulty deciding where your plot goes next, think in terms of disrupting a character's stable situation, thus surprising both reader and character and thereby triggering interest. An abrupt impact on a character's life is a great interest generator. Unanticipated upheaval, occurring when the character least expects it, can give that jagged plot line a sharp boost upward. This should not be an arbitrary intrusion, but an unexpected and yet indigenous barrier in the story's flow.

To Plot Or Not To Plot

Some people who yearn for a trip downstream simply jump in the boat and go with the flow — without plotting tools such as maps. Perhaps it is more fun to start this way. But probably it will require several trips down the stream to learn to avoid the sandbars and other obstacles underwater. The best way, ultimately, is to plot. It will take a little longer to organize your trip, jot down points of interest, and outline a safe advance from point to point. But most travelers seem to have better luck the plotted way.

The Primary Task With Fiction Is To Make The Reader Believe That The Story Is True

Details scattered throughout your story will help convince your reader that your story is real. For instance, you can tell someone that you dined in a restaurant that turns 360 degrees during your meal. But to really convince your reader, tell him that you first found yourself looking east across Lake Michigan toward lights on the Indiana Dunes, then north past Lincoln Park to Evanston and Skokie, west along Roosevelt Road toward Aurora, and south to Harvey and Chicago Heights. The reader should now believe you, at least more than before.

If A Chunk Of Information Is Important Enough For Inclusion In A Story, It Probably Deserves A Brief Scene To Show It

Say, for example, that your protagonist is parachuting from a burning aircraft onto a lush tropical island. The author can take several paragraphs to describe the island, but probably it will be much more effective to have the protagonist land and experience the island firsthand as he staggers for help.

PLOTTING CATEGORY STORIES

Plotting A Mystery By Using Two Perpetrators

Some authors approach their mystery by using two perpetrators, thus plotting it twice. First they start with a perpetrator and a motive. Then the author thinks of someone else who could have done it, and so the author starts over and plots it using the second perpetrator. For those who try it, this second version frequently illuminates and sometimes even replaces the first.

In A Murder Mystery Two Of The Most Successful Clues Involve Time Of A Crime And Access To It

Your suspect's access to the crime and whereabouts at the time of the crime are as important as the suspect's motives. For example, the author decides to include one of the victim's brothers-in-law, who flew in arms for the Nicaraguans during the Cold War. But the pilot's airplane crashes in the Nicaraguan jungle at the same time a crime is committed in Philadelphia in the USA. The brother-in-law may have hated the victim thoroughly but couldn't have been in the Nicaraguan underbrush and the Philadelphia subway at the same time. So the author drops this colorful pilot as rapidly as the pilot's plane had dropped into the Nicaraguan jungle.

The Disappearing Suspect

An interest-building technique in mystery writing can be to have a suspect disappear. In addition to increased uncertainty, this makes him increasingly suspect.

Modern Mystery Authors Have Fewer Suspects

In mysteries a half century ago the tendency was for the author to suspect everyone at least once. This assured the reader at least as many peaks of interest. But modern mystery writers have outgrown that approach. Today's authors give closer scrutiny to the characters' backgrounds — from physical to paranormal — and so the sleuth meets fewer suspects in his search for the guilty.

A Male-Female Story Paralleling A Mystery To Be Solved

Here is another approach to plotting your mystery novel along double tracks. In this case, on one track is your train featuring the mystery and on the other is your train featuring conflict between a male and a female. Such double tracks can provide a most rewarding trip.

Expecting Something Bad To Happen Is Typically More Captivating Than The Violence Itself

If the reader of a murder mystery thinks that something terrible is going to happen soon, he will keep turning pages. The building up to the violence can be much more sinister than the actual violence. Worrying about what may happen is usually much more captivating than what actually happens. Though the reader may sense danger, his excitement comes from not knowing until the trap door falls that indeed it will. What could sustain fear more than a prisoner being locked up next to an electric chair with his name on it? The sound of a door opening or a window breaking can be at least as frightening as the sight of the intruder himself. Topped only by an actual murder, the *threat* of murder guarantees sustained suspense.

A Detective's Unique Sense Of Justice

The hallmark of private-eye novels is the detective's unique sense of justice.

The Detective And Other Characters Meet Apart From Sleuthing

Personal camaraderie or clashes, apart from the sleuth's investigation, tend to make the sleuth and the characters more intriguing when they encounter each other officially.

Sleuth Asks Questions And Looks For Clues

The sleuth, forming initial impressions of the suspects and subtly or less than subtly investigating them, will do so by asking questions and personally investigating backgrounds of suspects most likely to have done the murder. Most suspects will proffer logical alibis when the sleuth first meets them. In a mystery novel the sleuth alternates between ferreting out information from suspects and finding and interpreting clues.

Basic Rule For Writing Romances

In writing romance fiction there is one basic rule: focus on the heroine first, then on the hero.

Detailed Plotting Of A Romance Novel

This is how some very successful romance writers plot their stories. After deciding the story theme, and jotting it down, these authors think of a crucial situation with which to open their story. This is the difficulty that the heroine faces as the story opens, and it is a difficulty that she ultimately must overcome in the story. The problem can be anything, ranging from the offer of a dangerous position with an overseas firm to being fired from her stateside job. Or perhaps she meets a long-lost lover after many years' absence, or her husband proves unfaithful and leaves permanently. This crucial situation leads into a conflict situation, such conflict foisted by other characters. The sum of those two situations, plus a resolution of the crucial situation and conflict situations, equals the plot. In other words, in these successful romance stories the crucial situations + conflict situations + resolution = a successful plot.

Ideally the opening crucial situation is revealed in no more than two or three opening paragraphs. The paragraphs can feature either author summary, or dialogue, or action, or introspection. This depends upon whether the author wants to emphasize, in addition to the crucial problem, some aspect such as character or mood or tone or setting. If the heroine is an introspective type, the opening paragraphs can feature the character's introspection. If an active person, they can feature action. If a gregarious person, they can feature dialogue. If the setting is a crucial part of the problem, such as the heroine needing to leave her poverty background, then an impoverished setting can be featured. Yes, the opening points in a story accomplish much. As literary types have stated over the years, "An author has two pages to hook an editor but only one to hook a reader."

The crucial situation needs enough staying power to last throughout the story or it must lead into another crucial situation directly downstream from the first. For continuity, the new crucial situation must arise naturally out of the original or preceding one.

Resurgence Of The Western Novel

The western novel, as with other category fiction, has had up and down eras. Today the Western is riding high. Western plots date back to the dime novels of the 1880s that featured gunmen hired to bring order if not law to the burgeoning territory. In the 1890s pulp magazines picked up such story-telling begun in the dime novels. Then the genre graduated into large novels, and in 1902 the landmark publication of *THE VIRGINIAN* resulted in a sale of more than a million copies. A decade later, 1912, saw publication of Zane Grey's *RIDERS OF THE PURPLE SAGE*, still the most famous western. Since then authors such as Luke Short and Louis L'Amour rank at the top of novelists whose sales of western books have been in the millions.

The cowboys and lawmen of the Old West assumed epic proportions because they filled a huge void. Frontier life found itself hundreds of centuries and thousand of miles from epic legends such as Saint George and the Dragon and King Arthur. Into this void stepped fabled Western lawmen such as Wyatt Earp and Doc Holliday, and words such as High Noon and the O.

K. Corral. The names of famous Western plots and characters, lawmen and villains, continue to intrigue fans throughout the world.

The heyday of the Old West covered a half century, from 1840 to 1890. In this relatively short time settlers claimed half a continent. The writer of Westerns should immerse himself in the history of this era, reading nonfiction works about the era and the area. In addition he should read critically (looking for techniques) in the works of credible Western fiction authors, for example A. B. Guthrie's *THE BIG SKY*. Reading in the genre should be a must for writers aspiring to perfect the Western formula. And speaking of formula, here are the basic half dozen plots that many writers feel cover the Western category: 1. the struggle against Indian story; 2. the lawman story; 3. the outlaw story; 4. the ranch story; 5. the revenge story; 6. and the range war story. Many good writers study stories written by another, add their own twists, and come up with plots of their own that are at least commercially successful.

The Traditional Western

The Traditional Western is one of four major types that Western authors are writing successfully. The Traditional Western deals with the basic Old West in terms of good versus evil, the hired gunman slaying the outlaw. These stories, somewhere around 65,000 words, have relatively few characters and are limited to a simple, straightforward plot.

The Historical Western

The second category is the Historical Western, often more than 100,000 words. Some of these stories feature actual historical figures of the Old West, while other authors limit these actual historical figures to secondary roles. These Historical Westerns do not rewrite history, and in fact the best ones stress authenticity, featuring a large degree of accuracy concerning conditions in the Old West.

The Young Adult Western

These stories are for readers aged nine or ten to fifteen, and today this is an inviting category. These short novels, covering around 30,000 words, are widely read by reviewers as well as young adults. The writers should remember that girls as well as boys peopled the plains of the Old West, that they too helped fend off outlaws trying to steal the family's cattle, or prohibited rustlers from cutting barbed wire, or outwitted attackers during Indian raids.

Adult Westerns

The final category is Adult Westerns, as in Adult Bookstores. This typically is for those authors who feel that sex will help them sell their stories, meanwhile ignoring the fact that almost all of the greatest writers of the past managed without gratuitous violence or graphic sex. For obvious reasons, many of these modern Adult Westerns are written under pseudonyms. Publishers themselves own the better known lines, often with one or two authors working "in-house" on a series.

Science Fiction Offers An Expanding Frontier For Writers

For those writers willing to study and disseminate the science technology indigenous in this genre, science fiction plots can be most rewarding. If a writer will study the scientific technology that is a mainstay of this category, and communicate it clearly to the reader, he will find editors and readers eagerly waiting to read whatever short or long fiction he writes. In addition to commercial opportunities available to good writers of science fiction, such writers can enjoy the excitement of claiming stars and galaxies for stage props. Other fiction is earth-oriented, but science fiction deals with all of creation in space and time. In a good science fiction story, the writer can experiment with a new world he creates in a new universe; he can write about the distant future or the distant past. The limitless arena of science fiction is an intriguing vista tailormade for the author "adequately gened" with imagination.

A Strong Market For Adventure Novels

New threats to civilized society keep emerging in the form of terrorism attacks, hostage-taking, and gang violence, and society's lack of a better response keeps producing fictional adventure heroes who are effective. Readers find themselves with such an urge to escape from society's inept response to violence, many are willing to escape to preposterous and otherwise unbelievable adventure heroes such as James Bond. Though the pulp market for short pieces has essentially disappeared, adventure books continue to be a lucrative market for writers. Many readers are interested in war and paramilitary and police activities, and a number of adventure writers are veterans of some such activity.

It is estimated that 80 percent of book readers in general are women but that 80 percent of adventure readers are men. Women's involvement in adventure reading and writing is beginning to change, however, as more and more women seem destined to end the twentieth century on a more equal footing with men.

Understandably, more and more strong characters in stories are women. In fact, a relatively new subdivision in adventure writing is Adult Westerns, with women authors and women characters riding ever higher in the saddle.

Many Adventure Writers Start With Plotting Rather Than Characters

By definition there is a tendency for adventure writers to emphasize plot outlining first, and only then write biographical sketches.

More Subjects For Adventure Writers

In addition to terrorism, weaponry, warfare, and gang violence, there have been basic themes for adventure authors over the centuries. As with mystery and horror and Westerns, revenge has been historic grist for many an adventure writer's grill. Such themes go back as far as Cain and Abel, with relatives or former friends pitted against each other. In the hundred or so major titles and offshoot titles in *THE EXECUTIONER* adventure series, a strong catalyst for protagonist Mack Bolan is revenge.

A Plot Formula For Adventure Novels

A plot formula for adventure novels, as with allied genre, could be: (1) a real trouble-making threat from an antagonist confronts a strong protagonist, (2) leading to a hectic pursuit, (3) resolved through one or more violent confrontations.

Horror Stories

A recognized master of the horror story, Stephen King employs a master's touch in making supernatural stories believable. One of his widely emulated techniques is the insertion of familiar brand-name objects. In fact, parts of some stories written by emulators now read like a grocery list, it is claimed.

BEGIN YOUR STORY IN WRITING IN EARNEST

To Open Your Story Have Your Main Character Facing A Major Problem

A dependable way to begin a piece of fiction is with a main character facing a problem that both the character and the reader want to be solved. The problem facing this main character should be important and not easily overcome. If your main character is your hero, he must *deserve* to overcome his difficulty. If he's a villain he must *deserve* to face ultimate defeat. Whether hero or villain, he should prove his mettle through facing and overcoming formidable obstacles—ultimately winning or losing after displaying great courage on stormy seas.

As you open your story, give your character or characters an emotional crisis. Your reader can most easily identify with a character if you introduce your protagonist, or whomever, with a problem that the reader reacts to emotionally from the start. Following are some examples:

A character's spouse has just been killed by an assailant, and the character suffers grief, and the reader pities him.

The doorbell rings, and the van from American Family Sweepstakes has arrived bringing the character ten million dollars. The reader sympathizes with the character's indecision as the character faces various demands for the money.

A character has been counting the vote tally on the large board and realizes he has just been elected the state's next governor. In addition to sharing his exuberation, the reader considers with the governor the looming challenges of running the state.

Sherlock Holmes suddenly finds himself with a tough case to solve. The reader shares his excitement in approaching the problem.

Nicholas, in *WAR AND PEACE,* is endangered by approaching conflict between the Emperor and Czar, and the reader can readily identify with a problem that can happen to the reader if his own government is threatened.

The Reader Must Participate As Well As Sympathize And Identify

The reader must do more than sympathize and identify with the character's emotional crisis presented at the start of a story. The reader must participate in the character's decision-making process. If the reader is thinking, "Play it smart, George; ask the police to help you solve your wife's murder" or "George, the local police are inept and maybe corrupt and what you need is a private detective," the reader can identify with the character. The reader has empathy with a character when the reader pulls for the character to make the right decision.

Situations Featuring Injustice Or Disguise Are Successful Story Openers

Some opening situations, for example those involving lynchings in the old South, are proven winners. Another features a couple of strangers, dressed like repairmen, dropping in to use your phone.

Some Openings Present The Protagonist's Problem More Subtly

Though it is good to start a story with a protagonist facing a major problem, it is not always necessary to hit the reader over the head with the fact. Sometimes the opening few sentences or paragraphs set a stage that features not the protagonist's explicit problem, but instead the story's setting or tone or atmosphere or perhaps all three. Then onto this stage steps the protagonist who reveals the first of many interesting characteristics that point weakly or strongly to his dilemma, his predicament, his problem.

Conflict Should Appear Near The Opening Of A Story

The opening pages of every story should present the emotional conflict within the protagonist's mind: first drive versus second drive, fear versus duty, tranquility versus revenge, courage versus danger. Normally, whatever it was that caused the protagonist's inner conflict should have been in place before the story opens; for example Hamlet's indecision, Abraham's love for his son, the master spy's zealous bent, Robin Hood's individualistic nature. It is, of course, possible to tell an outstanding story that opens by describing the development of the first drive and the second drive in the protagonist's mind. But normally, again, the story opening should be concerned with the conflict brought about by the arrival of the second drive. Normally reader interest concerns resolution of the problem instead of its origins. Before many paragraphs or pages the reader needs to see the protagonist handling the problem brought about by the meeting of both drives.

Story Openings Are Important Enough To Merit A Number Of Rewrites

Story beginnings, like story endings, are strong candidates for a number of rewrites. The opening of a story is the story's most important gambit and thus the area most worthy of attention. The opening should hook the reader and at the same time establish the setting and introduce or at least suggest the type of characters and mood and tone in the story. It is axiomatic that many successful authors rewrite openings many times.

Opening A Story With A Scene

Stories opening with a scene have some advantage over those opening with a summary. A story opening with a scene immediately catches the reader's interest as he finds himself involved with one or more characters. Opening with a scene does have the disadvantage, however, of the reader's being unprepared to see what is significant in the scene. Opening scenes can startle the unprepared reader and suggest expectations that the story cannot meet. But this risk normally is not a serious one. The writer can clarify in his subsequent paragraphs ambiguities left from the opening.

Two Kinds Of Story Openings

There are two schools of thought regarding the best way to open a story. In one school, the "attention grabbing approach," the author tries to gain the reader's attention immediately—to open with a sentence or two so intriguing the reader will feel compelled to continue with the story. The other opening is the "build-up approach."

Here is an example of the attention-grabbing opening:

> "By Jove," said the duchess, flicking ashes from her cigar. "I think I'd prefer, sir, that you get your hand off my knee."

But a criticism of the preceding approach is that no matter how much your story comes on like gang-busters, your reader may find it difficult to be interested in absolute strangers. In addition, some readers may resent being startled by a story that comes on too strong.

Here is an example of the build-up opening:

> The Victorian sofa squeaked as the duchess claimed occupancy. She turned sideways, eyeing her companion or was it her cigar? Someone coughed several times. A nearby male hand levitated from ashes.

If the event involves some unusual behavior on the part of the opening characters, there might be a need to show by comparison how the characters react under normal circumstances.

The trend may be tilting toward the attention-grabbing approach for openers, television competition being what it is in terms of capturing viewers' attention. But even the attention-getting opening should contain enough information. Certainly it is important to give the reader at least a hint as to what kind of story is about to unfold. If it is going to be humorous, don't start with a funeral. If an execution, don't start with a joke.

Authors Play Host To Readers

Some authors begin a story by considering themselves to be a courteous host and the reader a first-time guest, the author introducing the guest to one or two people at a time. After a brief acquaintanceship the host moves the guest to a new introduction.

Opening Should Identify The Story

If the opening of the story doesn't give the reader a clue as to what the story is about, the chances are he will not turn to the next page.

Narration Ill-Defined

Webster begins a definition of narration with this: "To tell (as in a story) in detail." As we begin our story we may well question Webster's definition (or anyone else's) of this important literary term. What of the story-teller who narrates in generalities or highlights rather than details? In literature, according to usage, everything in a story is narrative except action, reaction, dialogue, and introspection.

Make Your Characters Show

Show through the use of action scenes instead of just telling about your characters. Narration is most susceptible to too much telling instead of showing.

Dialogue Can Make A Good Story Opening

"She can't spend all that money in a lifetime," Diane said. Or, "What terrible accident—where?" Joan cried. But care should be taken not to proceed too far into the story before explaining such attention-getting dialogue.

Almost Always It's Better To Show Than To Tell

Poor: "It looks as cold as all get-out outside." Better, "Her fingers were sticking to the window pane."

Speaker Paragraph

In dialogue give each speaker a new paragraph.

Don't Double-Identify Your Speaker

Poor: Ralph found the airplane ride his most exciting experience. "Never had so much excitement in my life," he said.

Better: Ralph found the airplane ride his most exciting experience. "Never had so much excitement in my life." (Omit *he said.*)

Don't Make Your Characters Do The Impossible

Don't write, "Funniest thing I ever heard," he laughed. He couldn't speak and laugh at the same time. Instead, "Funniest thing I ever heard." (Period). He laughed. Of course, don't have someone's eyes sweep across the floor, when it's so easy to have a gaze move, to say nothing of a broom sweep. Neither is it better to write that someone's eyes rolled across the countryside.

Don't Duplicate Real Life Speech

It is important to remember that in writing dialogue we do *not* want to duplicate real speech. For one thing, real speech is straightforward for the most part. In good fiction, dialogue frequently is indirect. And often in the process your character will show more wit, or erudition, or cleverness than in real life. Real speech is relatively dull. At least every few sentences of your fictional dialogue should cause your reader to say to himself, "I wish when I talk I could make a remark like that." For example: "A child considered cute by his parents is apt to get cut by his playmates," or "It has been my experience that the boss who speaks of his employees as 'My men' or 'My women' flatters himself" or "Since seeing is believing, then isn't believing seeing? or "The harder I work the luckier I get."

Scenes Need Increasing Conflict

As with the main story itself, each scene should begin at a low point of tension and rise to a point of high tension, followed by a resolution. The Drogues and the Drags began bad-mouthing each other at gang meetings, and word swept through the neighborhood. They met at a street corner, began battle, and the resolution came with the arrival of police.

The conflict in a scene need not be the same as the story's main conflict. In the gang-fight scene, the main story conflict might be between the mayor and the city council concerning how to handle gangs. Obviously when you begin a scene in the middle, as with the gang shootout, you've avoided some possibly dull preliminaries.

One Scene Can Flow Into Another

Though the street-corner fight ends with the arrival of the police, and with the police comes the scene's climax and resolution, perhaps some of the gang members escape to resume battle elsewhere. Thus the conflict carries over from that scene to an ensuing scene.

Plan Your Characters' Dialogue So They Don't Sound Dull

Your characters should and can display more wit and learning in their dialogue because you, their author, have time to sit back and think about what they say. How many times after talking with someone have you thought of a word or words you might have used? Your characters talk better because you have time.

Using Too Much Information To Begin A Story

There is too often a tendency among professional as well as novice authors to cram an opening with information better saved until later. Realizing that we need early-on to introduce our main characters as believable, we burden the reader with paragraphs and even pages of background information in the first chapter. In doing this we are apt to overwhelm the reader either with author summary or dialogue or character introspection. Most of the time the better way to begin the story is with a crucial conflict situation, the protagonist having already arrived, confronting the conflict. Then we can sprinkle in some background information either through dialogue or introspection. Certainly we need to know something about the protagonist early in the story, but we can learn this in part by seeing his reaction to the opening conflict situation.

Two Ways To Tell A Story Dramatically

Stories can be revealed in two ways: author summary or scenes. In author summaries the author tells. In scenes the author shows. Scenes, ideally, comprise most of our stories. But author summaries can of course present a change of pace as well as a capsule method of informing the reader.

Opening Scene Affects Protagonist Permanently

It is important to remember that the crucial opening situation in a story should show how decisions made this day are going to affect the protagonist from now on.

A Character's Heredity And Environment

A character's ancestors and economic background are major influences in shaping his life. Many successful authors can suggest much background with a few details or during the crucial opening scene. Does the heroine want to succeed because her parents had menial jobs in the town factory? Dickens and Horatio Alger wore this one out, eh? Well, President Bill Clinton campaigned in part on the basis that he deserved the minority vote because of a youthful country-store association with minorities in the South. There are many intriguing variations in which backgrounds are important to story lines.

Story Peaks And Valleys

Strong action scenes are considered peaks in a story. Between the peaks come rest and relaxation in the valleys as the author summarizes or presents author introspection.

Three Kinds Of Story Openings

There are three schools of thought concerning the best way for writers to open a story. Some writers believe that the action must come first before the characters and the setting. Others feel just as strongly that we should get to know our characters first. A third school is convinced that we should set the stage before bringing on either characters or action. Often the type of story the author is telling is the deciding factor as to how a story opens. A western novel frequently opens with action, a mystery with character or setting or action, a romance with character, and a long mainline novel with setting.

Stories that open with character emphasis appear to be most successful most often. People instinctively are interested in people. However, opening with character emphasis, as we know, doesn't mean that we start with one or more character biographies--not even the protagonist's. For example, we don't need to know in the first few pages who his parents are, where he was born, his attitude about abortion (unless a heroine is heading to a Right-To-Life demonstration), or his relationship to other characters. But we must understand how the protagonist feels at the moment. When we understand why a character feels as he or she does, we can more closely sympathize with them. Why should we care which side of an abortion demonstration our protagonist joins if we don't care about her? We writers have only about a page for our readers to start caring about one or more characters, or at least to experience an awakening interest.

As we open a story by featuring character, this does not necessarily mean physical description of a character. An early indication of a person's sex and age and physique usually is enough. Details, such as the color of a person's hair or eyes or other characteristics, can be scattered throughout the book.

The First Things In A Story's Opening Chapters

In climbing the literary ladder with a successful story we should consider covering the following subjects in the opening chapters: problem, concern about the problem, decision, action, and evaluation. (This is the old setting, scene, summary formula—with the setting less massaged these days.) When another main character, perhaps the villain, enters the story with opposing attitudes, we have added an ingredient for increasing drama at or near the start of the story.

More And More Emphasis On Scenes In A Story

An important reminder. Thanks to the influence of movies and television, readers have become increasingly accustomed to recognizing a story as a series of scenes. Modern authors rely primarily on scenes to put their stories across.

Normally It Is A Good Idea To Start Your Story By Making Your Protagonist, Even If A Villain, Likeable

In *EYE OF THE NEEDLE,* the World War II spy from Nazi Germany begins as a hardworking bicyclist making his way through London's wartime traffic and then familiar boarding house setting. Then in his room he abruptly commits his first of many murders. Typically it is a good idea to start your story by making even a villain likable, despite any early indication that he won't become Mr. Personality.

In Storytelling Never Solve A Problem For The Reader Without Raising At Least One More

Your story's unsolved problems keep the reader turning pages.

Give Your Names File One More Check

This is one of your most neglected yet most important lists. Keep it handy so you can change it as needed as you write your story. It contains not only the names of your characters—as a handy reference apart from your character sketches—but also the names of countries, states, cities, villages, streets, swamps, rivers, beaches, highways, hotels, restaurants, and so forth. You will surely be rewarded if you jot down more than you have to refer back to. This list can even be a reference as you tell future tales.

Also Create An Ideas File For Your Story

As you write a story, also maintain an ideas file using cards or notebook or computer. This can include everything from lines of dialogue that come to mind to ideas for setting or plots or major and minor scenes.

SPECIAL BEGINNING FOR CATEGORY STORY

Murder Mysteries

In a mystery novel the reader should discover in your opening pages a murder that is happening or a murder that is about to happen. Fear will come later.

Also, early in your mystery your characters should show shock as a result of the crime. The crime has shattered their normal living, and permeating the opening chapter is a story of gravity that results from murder—in particular inexplicable murder. You, the author, have shaken your characters' world, and so now you must help your characters steady it. Typically the author does this first by introducing those characters who seem closest to the murder, and also bringing in the protagonist to take charge of the matter. So your protagonist takes charge and begins to steady the world. Having now introduced the victim, those most affected by the crime, and the protagonist, you are ready to move with your story into the middle one-third of your book.

Begin your story at the time of murder or soon after, with the sleuth looking into the victim's background for the motive. Very quickly bring the sleuth into contact with both the innocent and the guilty. The sleuth will delve into character backgrounds to see if there was an opportunity for murder. Again, opportunity is as important as motive.

DOUBLE CHECKS MIDWAY THROUGH YOUR STORY

"Keeping Your Readers With You"

Facts Reinforce Fiction

Factual information not only satisfies the reader's curiosity, it also strengthens the illusion that your story is as real as the reader's real world.

Beware Of The -Ly Word

Too many writers tend to use too many -ly words, in particular in dialogue. For example: "She said *sarcastically.* She said *flippantly;* She said *spritely.* " In the great majority of cases, use of -ly, most often with dialogue, can be avoided. There are a few exceptions, but these are almost entirely those adverbs that clarify the verb *said* (in contrast to attempts to clarify the dialogue). It is all right to write, "She said distinctly" or "She said loudly." This of course clarifies her speech, not her emotion. But almost always we should avoid such usage as, "He said tersely" or He said flippantly." In these cases the dialogue should speak for itself.

Almost Always The Correct Verb Is *Said*

In describing who is speaking when you use dialogue, almost always use *said.* Do not write, "Go get it," he *ordered* or *"*Hand it over," he *demanded* or "Are you ready?" he asked. The explanatory verbs are unnecessary. The dialogue brings the message. The *only* reason to explain anything with the dialogue is to identify the speaker. If this is necessary, merely use the verb said. "Go get it," he said, and so forth. There are even worst-case examples of using verbs other than said. For example, "Give me your money," he *growled. "*I like it," he *smiled.* These call for impossible feats from the character, and they draw attention from the dialogue. You want your reader to listen to your dialogue, not your technique for getting it to him. (These cautions are raised even though most of the preceding words are not in the same room with, "Her eyes rolled over the carpet" and similar impossibilities cited earlier. It is appropriate to strive for the correct verb for the action, but in almost all cases the correct verb is said.

Identify The Speaker Later In The Sentence

Do not open a *paragraph* of dialogue with speaker identification. Rather, begin a paragraph with dialogue and then identify the speaker in the first break in the first sentence. "Let's go shopping," she said, "this money is burning a hole in my purse."

Beware Of *Said She*

Place the character's name first in reader identification. "Go with it," Mary said. Not "Go with it," said Mary. Though various authors use the "said Mary," its use is more and more considered old-fashioned. "Prithee," said he, "whist goest thee?" Rather, in more modern writing, "You're going where?" he said.

Monotonous *Saids*

If your "saids" are becoming monotonous, you can always interrupt them with character actions:

POOR

"Baby Ray had a dog," Big Sister said.
"Baby Ray loved his dog," Big Brother said.
"And his dog loved Baby Ray," Big Mother said.

BETTER

"Baby Ray had a dog," Big Sister said.
"Baby Ray loved his dog," Big Brother said.
Big Mother smiled. "And his dog loved Baby Ray."

Reader And Story Must Travel At The Same Pace

Do not let your story leave your reader behind. Neither should you let your reader get ahead of your story. You and your reader must travel through the story at the same speed. Do not slow your action with detailed flashbacks or foreshadowing when the immediate action should be the center of attention.

Selecting Details

The ability to select details with care is one of the most valuable skills in both fiction and nonfiction writing. It is the same as selecting details if a girlfriend or boyfriend or a cautious fiance asks us to tell them something about ourselves. We could start with our childhood and relate everything we remember that happened to us, but, of course, we shouldn't. Unless we really want to bore our acquaintance, we select that one pep rally in primary or secondary school, or that blind date in college—we carefully limit our past by citing only those meaningful allusions that suggest the real us. We control what we choose to reveal in order to illuminate what we want illuminated.

Avoid Lumps Of Character Biographical Information

Often those lumps of character biographical information can be eliminated or postponed until later and then diffused. How much of this information will your reader need in order to understand your story at this point? If needed later, at what most likely point in the story? Again, don't grab your reader by the collar and say, "This may not take long, but listen."

Suspense Begins When Your Character Is Forced To Take Action

Whenever a character is _forced_ to take action—no matter what the reason—the scene is tailor-made for holding the reader's attention.

Make Your Characters Love Someone Or Something In Addition To Themselves

In order to make readers care about characters, however bad, it can be helpful to make them love someone or even something. For example a dog or a cat or a horse.

CONSTANT LOGGING OF SCENES AND SUMMARIES

Viewpoint In A Scene

How quickly in a scene do you establish the point of view? Where is the first point that your reader knows unequivocally who is telling the story?

Purpose Of A Scene

If a scene tends to get lost in the shuffle in your story, then ask yourself, "What is the purpose of this scene?" If you can think of none, then maybe the scene doesn't belong in the story.

Visualizing Scenes

Scenes usually have settings in precise locations that the reader can visualize. In former years—in the era of large eyeglasses perhaps—authors often described the scenes in exhaustive detail. Your modern author aims mainly for the high spots, giving the readers only enough details to help them visualize the story.

A Story's Two Main Parts

The two basic parts of a story are scenes and summaries. Your typical scene has specific settings and characters and dialogue. Since scenes usually are harder to write than summaries, most authors rely too heavily on summaries to tell their stories. But most scenes grip your reader tighter than do summaries. You want to pull your readers into the world you've created, making them feel as if they belong in it. You do this most effectively by letting the readers participate in this world firsthand. You take your readers into the scene, giving them something they can picture. In scenes, events come to the reader as they happen instead of after-the-fact.

Though scenes almost always are more engaging than summaries—and often you improve your story-telling by converting summaries into scenes—you of course still need some summaries, however brief. Perhaps the point of the scene is too difficult to make in the scene itself. Also, summaries can vary the rhythm of your writing. Scene after scene without a break might make your reader feel punch drunk, especially if you write intense, brief scenes. It could resemble a long ride on a fast train. Now and then you want to slow, as Amtrak does for a depot, giving your reader an opportunity to rest between rounds. Summarization can indeed accomplish this. An author of one of the estimated twenty-million manuscripts unpublished each year in the U. S. had this recent observation:

> "I'd always heard that the proper order in telling a story is setting and then scene and then summary. Now they're saying that because of television, readers are expecting one scene after another, with the scene swallowing up the setting and summary. So I wrote a 40,000-word novelette, using a chain of scenes one or two pages long, but my husband just told me it reads like I'm firing an assault weapon."

Or riding a fast train on a long track with the stations blurred, if at all visible. In her rapidly-fired scenes, her characters met, argued or loved, and then parted. Her plot, characterization, setting, and dialogue were all passable, but the never-ending scenes proved too monotonous. In her latest revision, for starters, she is combining a few of the shorter scenes into longer ones. And she is making scattered use of summaries.

Emotions Should Intensify In Each Scene

Action or conflict should increase in your story's every scene. The emotions of both your protagonist and your antagonist should grow increasingly more intense in each scene. For example, they might increase through these emotional stages: irritation or annoyance; to beginning anger; to powerful anger; to anger in which the character goes berserk. Almost never should the character jump all the way from annoyance to going berserk; it's simply too abrupt. To gauge your novel's rising conflict, judge your character's emotional level at the start of a scene compared to the end of the scene. You need a step-by-step increase in your character's emotional involvement. This applies to every scene. The character is fully revealed to the reader when the reader sees him acting or reacting through emotional stages of increasing intensity. Your characters should change emotionally a little at a time as your conflict unfolds, with the conflict rising slowly, but inexorably rising.

For a fuller (and better) description of appropriate ways to present increasing stages of emotional level in a scene, the author should check the bibliography later in this book. A number of books include help with this technique.

Summaries Can Be Useful In Avoiding Repetitive Writing

For example, let's assume that there is a dock strike and each time your hero launches his boat he gets clobbered. Unless you're the hero this eventually could seem repetitive if not monotonous. But if you summarize some of these attacks—in other words, have them happen offstage—then the scene in which he returns to blow up the dock will have real punch.

Story Elements Too Minor To Justify A Scene

An element should be important enough to justify a scene. If the element involves only minor settings or minor characters, it might be best to summarize, and thus give the succeeding scene more power by contrast.

Authors Help Readers Share Characters' Experiences

The best storytellers usually do more than just say, "Jean gave someone a million dollars" or "Susan climbed Pike's Peak" or "Paul dusted his mother with an uppercut." In the best story-telling, the authors strive to let the readers share the experiences—normally preferring scenes to summaries. These authors prefer brief emotional revelations to briefer summarizations.

Avoid Long Introductions To A Scene

Poor: He must hurry and catch this bus. If he didn't deliver his ransom money on time, the kidnappers might carry out their threat.

Better: He leaped into the bus, clutching his satchel. Could he meet that ransom deadline?

Close Out Your Scenes

Normally do not skip from scene to scene without some summarization.

Showing And Telling

If we tell someone we have a new wristwatch, but refuse to show it, we could soon stand alone. As for Jean, again, it is not enough to say that she was generous. It's better to show her giving someone a million dollars. Instead of declaring Susan bold, we can show her climbing Pike's Peak. If Paul is angry, we can show him tagging his mother with an uppercut, perhaps. To make this action even more believable, we should show the recipient's grin as Jean counts out a million dollars. And we can show the height of Pike's Peak as seen from straight up. Maybe Paul grew angry because his mother left some skates inside the front door to prevent his slipping in unannounced.

Details Add Credibility

Throughout life we use details to understand larger objects. We judge a person by his smile. Credibility comes from the use of details in writing, though the details should not endanger the story line.

Evading Another Character's Question Or Observation

Improper response, a technique well known to authors who write for stage and screen, can be effective in improving dialogue. A character either inadvertently or advertently gives the wrong answer to or ignores or otherwise evades another character's question or observation.

NORMAL DIALOGUE:

"You seem to know your way around. Have you been here before?"

"Yes. Several times."

EVASIVE RESPONSE:

"You seem to know your way around. Have you been here before?"

"It sure is interesting."

Or:

"This is one of the plushest golf resorts anywhere around."

"They do have a large club house."

Dialect To Be Avoided

Be wary of introducing dialect into your story. Dialect tends to draw the reader's attention away from your story, focusing instead on the means of getting the dialogue across.

Character Introspection

A major advantage of print fiction over film or stage is print-fiction's mind reading. Film and even stage fiction have some obvious advantages over print, but both fail in the major area of mind reading. So, and this should be no surprise, mind reading in fiction is so effective and easy (though not that easy to use well) many authors are prone to overuse it. Here is an example of overuse:

"You want me climbing down to rescue your husband?" Otto said. Otto hoped that his request sounded sincere. But surely she wasn't expecting him to risk his own neck to save her bat-brained mate.

"What can we do, Otto? What can we do?"

"Three hundred feet straight down. I'll try."
Otto again tried to sound sincere.

"But we can't lose you and him too." Otto
looked over the ledge. "Make that four hundred. He's
crazy. He must be part bat."

"I didn't marry him for his mind." It was great
to have her acknowledge it aloud. "But how can I
live with myself if he falls to his death?"

Otto suppressed a smile. His answer was too
easy. "You won't live alone, Mary. I'm a high-flying
eagle myself, not a bat."

You probably read the above as less than even. Too
many interruptions are just as irritating in a fictional scene
as we find them in real life, and the author has interrupted
his conversation again and again with personal, sometimes
bitter, insights. Just about every sentence is followed by
entry into Otto's mind. (Otto hoped that his request
sounded sincere). Even if these mind readings help clarify
the conversation, their number still jars the reader.
Explanations get in the way. Here is the scene improved
only by editing out the unnecessary explanation:

"You want me climbing down to rescue your
husband?" Otto said. But surely she wouldn't
expect him to risk his own neck.

"What can we do, Otto? What can we do?"

"Three hundred feet straight down. It may
sound bat-brained, but I'll try."

"Still, we can't lose you and him too."

Otto looked over the ledge. "Make that four
hundred. He's crazy. He must be part bat."

"I didn't marry him for his mind. But how can
I live with myself if he falls to his death?"

Otto suppressed a smile. "You won't live
alone, Mary. I'm a high-flying eagle, not a bat."

The point is, literary mind reading is an invaluable technique—within bounds. In the preceding scene we only give the reader an idea of what's going on inside Otto's mind—the repetitive explanations are gone. Introspection should not be overdone. In a dialogue scene, for instance, introspection should support dialogue, not do away with it.

Character Action Verbs

If you want your character action verbs to be unobtrusive, and you should, the simplest way is to delete them when you can:

> Should I let him drop? Maybe so, he thought.
> Should I let him drop? Maybe so.

Don't forget, character action verbs tell your reader who is speaking. Because each scene you write will be from a single point of view, you usually will find character identification superfluous.

Longer Passages Of Character Introspection Can Be Set Off

Longer passages of character introspection can be segregated in their own paragraphs, if desired. Here is an example:

> Otto stood near the edge of the ledge, though not precariously close. Was his offer to help sufficient? What to say when her husband fell? How could she think he'd risk his own neck? An autopsy, that must be it—she was rehearsing for one. Presumably Otto's, not his.

A Caution Against Long Introspection

Be on guard against long passages of introspection. They usually mean that you're telling your reader things that you should be showing. If you have Otto stand on the ledge and reflect for more than a few lines concerning his predicament (or more than a page if musing over things at the neighborhood bar), you can easily find your character narrating when he should be showing.

Certainly there are exceptions, however. You might want to describe a particular setting that especially impresses one of your characters. Or you may desire longer narration in order to introduce several characters in a batch. But as a durable yardstick, normally limit your character's introspections to no more than a page, breaking them up here and there or converting the entire reflection into one scene.

Good Dialogue Identifies Its Speaker

Ordinarily you should be able to lift dialogue at random from your manuscript and tell who is talking.

Speech Mannerisms

Be careful not to overuse speech mannerisms. It is not necessary to suggest an English accent, for example, throughout a person's dialogue. Even if your character normally would drop the h with every word, it is not required that he do so throughout the dialogue. If he drops the h once in every sentence or even paragraph, the reader will understand that he is English. The same applies if he talks mountaineeze. He only needs a few infrequent uses of "yaller" for "yellow" or "thar" for "there" or "fur" for "far" to establish his credentials.

Male And Female Dialogue

Try to show the contrast when a female is conversing with a male. Some writers maintain that women tend to speak from emotion whereas men speak from a desire for action. How often have you heard a woman relating an emotional story and the man asking for the bottom line?

Longer Sentences Suggest An Unhurried Mood—Shorter Sentences More Hurried Action

Compare, "Shall we go for a stroll through the park this afternoon?" to, "Let's do the park this afternoon." Or, "Once upon a time in the beautiful kingdom of Choo," to, "Once in Choo."

Terse Dialogue Can Advance A Story Rapidly

Compare, "The building's on fire" to simply yelling, "Fire!"

Dialogue And Introspection Make An Effective Combination

"Nancy, your son was star of the game. He's the main reason our team won." Nancy, of course, smiled at this. She agreed that her son was the star of the game, and she wasn't aware that anyone else played.

Dialogue, Introspection, And Narration Can Make An Even More Effective Combination

Variety is the spice of story-telling life as well as of regular life. The attention span of some of your readers will not be ideal. To help keep readers awake, break the monotony by fishing among dialogue and introspection and narration.

It Is Important To Read Dialogue Aloud

It can be helpful to read all your writing aloud, especially dialogue. After you have completed the first draft of a dialogue scene, it's a good idea to read it aloud to yourself or to someone else. Or perhaps even better, read it into a voice recorder and play it back.

Sparkling Dialogue

Though the attainment of sparkling dialogue is easier said (or written) than done, this valuable technique is learnable. Some authors find it helpful to jot down various lines of dialogue used in television stories they like. Sometimes they compare these with what they think the characters should have said. Some compare the lines to what they think characters would have said in real life. Of course, a study of dialogue in books is helpful.

Keeping A Reader With You As Your Plot Thickens

Let's say that partway through a murder mystery, for example, murder has been committed and the sleuth is centering his attention on the prime suspect. It looks as if your story will end in the middle. But instead of that you bring in a second murder. The prime suspect seemingly was not involved with the second victim. So now you have two murders and two suspects. The reader's interest is proportionally doubled. Who will get shot next? Even more, the reader is caught in the inner conflict of his sleuth as he decides which suspect to follow. A word of caution, however; avoid too much of a good thing. Experienced authors limit their murders to two or three, lest the reader begin to feel bored.

Reader Awareness

Do not keep from the reader a secret known by the sleuth.

No Matter How Likeable Or Even Admirable A Protagonist, He Must Have At Least One Glaring Weakness

Again, Hamlet's indecision. Or, in *EYE OF THE NEEDLE,* the German spy's allegiance to Nazi Germany.

Make Use Of Your Protagonist's Five Senses

Check your pages to make sure that they reflect full use of sensory reality. If a page has nothing except what your protagonist saw, or what he heard, rewrite that page to involve the sense of touch or taste or smell. It is uncanny how much an added sense can strengthen a story page-by-page.

Your Protagonist Develops A Series Of Problems

A major difference between your protagonist and other characters in your story is that the former has a series of problems. Other major characters may have one basic problem as the result of the conflict between the first and second drives. Minor characters need have no problems whatsoever. But the protagonist, with both inner and outer problems, has more than his share.

A Simple Formula Sometimes Used When Writing A Story

Some writers have stripped their plotting to this basic exercise: have three episodes in each chapter and a more dramatic scene (episode) every fifth chapter. Of course, this arbitrary rule is a simple guide that does not apply to every story. But if you use it as a guide, you should find it much easier to gauge the roll of the waves.

Present A New Problem Or At Least A New Question Every Few Pages

The reader is in the business of solving a character's problems. So the story should not solve a problem or answer a question without first raising at least one new question or problem. This means that the reader will eagerly turn pages to see what happens next.

Minor Plots Versus The Main Plot

Neither your characters nor your readers have time or need to stray far from the main story line. The course is ahead under a blazing sun as light pierces darkness at journey's end.

HARBOR NIGHTS

"Ending Your Story"

Story's Safe End

The most memorable last page of a story is one that leaves your reader feeling that the narrative still expands onward after the reader closes the book.

The "Obligatory Scene"

A scene at or very near the end of a story should feature a showdown between the forces that have been in conflict throughout the story. For example the Old West, where the bad guy shoots it out with the sheriff, or the New East, where the heroine gains control of the stock majority and fires her CEO husband. This is commonly known as the "obligatory scene."

Climax Is Protagonist's Biggest Hurdle

A story's climax scene is the biggest hurdle the hero or heroine must face. The author should play this scene out unstintingly. Readers want and deserve the satisfaction of experiencing a fully satisfying climax. Both your hero and your reader must be rewarded with a significant and satisfying climax scene; or if your protagonist is a villain, it must be important and satisfying that he receive his deserved punishment. If the protagonist is to win, the reward at the end should be appropriately rewarding. Failure should mean loss of life, or at the very least loss of something of great value.

Your climax is your hero's big test. Don't short-change your readers in the climax. Let your reader savor your climax to the fullest.

Abrupt Endings

Be on guard lest your ending be too abrupt. Some authors prefer to end their manuscript promptly after the climax. Other writers would rather add a final chapter to tie up all the strings, and to suggest what will be the characters' futures. Strive for common ground between making the ending too abrupt and belaboring it.

Readers' Rewards

After reading your story, your readers should be left with a feeling of enlightenment and entertainment as well as a new outlook on life. Do the characters and the story or both stay with the reader after he closes the book? Were the main characters and plot memorable?

Because about eighty percent of book readers are women, authors might well keep in mind what many women readers find rewarding. Many find psychological action more intriguing than physical. However, most good stories have a mixture of both, appealing to both sexes. Most likely your finished story should do the same.

Use Of A Jagged Line Can Indicate A Character's Progress Through A Story

To review a character's reward or punishment in any situation, some authors draw a "story line" that jags upward or downward, graphically depicting the character's situation at each point in the story.

Omitting Information

After completing your story, can you agree with Hemingway that what you left out of your novel was more than what you put into it. Further, can you agree with others that one percent of what they know about a subject goes into their story, the author imbuing himself with knowledge of the other ninety-nine percent?

In Most Contemporary Fiction, Characters Make Up Perhaps Seventy Percent Of The Story, And The Plot The Other Thirty Percent

If a story fails, look first to see if the characters have failed to come to life. Perhaps a character is lifeless because he has no flaws. If the author has shown a character without flaws, then he has not shown that character through the eyes of the other characters. Perhaps the central question raised by the story has not been answered. Maybe the plot was too thin to carry the story's length, or so elaborate the reader is left confused.

Follow-up Characteristics

If the author shows a character with an identifying characteristic, such as a speech dialect or a profession, that characteristic should be consistent throughout the story. If you mention that someone is a barber, be sure and let him cut someone's hair before the story is finished, or at least let him open his shop.

End Of The Game And The Story

We should hope to end the story as we would a successful chess game. A chess game and a story both have their darkest moments as the end nears. In chess a player faces checkmate, loss of the game, and in a story the protagonist also faces defeat. This "Darkest Moment" is a phrase sometimes used in literature and apropos to chess. Preceding the darkest moment is a major move or a major scene in which it seems that the protagonist will win. But instead, bang! Your chess opponent or your story's villain comes in from the blind side for the coup de grace. Checkmate for the good guys, or at least for the protagonists, now looks unavoidable. The villain has a gun pointed at the protagonist's head. But then with startling surprise the chess master sweeps in with his Queen and cries "Checkmate" toward his opponent's bedraggled King. Or if it's High Noon and the protagonist and villain approach each other, then the protagonist steps into shadows and fires the fatal blow from a safe gray area as the blinded villain stares for the final time.

Following this Darkest Moment there can be additional scenes of conflict. The losing chess player may glare or even refuse to turn his king piece sideways as he's supposed to in defeat. An angry town council may still await the marshal, the council eager for a new face behind the badge. And this builds until the absolute final resolution at the end.

Webster's Definition Of Story Climax

Webster defines climax as "b: the point of highest dramatic tension or a major turning point in the action (as of a play)." According to this definition, certainly, both the chess player and the marshal have qualified.

Story Closing

After the climax, your reader needs a few paragraphs or pages to settle down from the experience before leaving your story. This can be presented in a brief author summary or scene that suggests life expanding beyond the last page.

Do Not Drag Out Your Story

Again, remember to stop when you're through. Don't add paragraph upon paragraph after you've already given the answers.

Rewriting Separates The Chaff From The Wheat

Revise your manuscript until it reads like what you'd want to read as a reader rather than what you'd like to write as a writer.

The Uncluttered Climax

The author should not clutter a climactic scene by explaining loose ends that should have been explained earlier. This is especially true of the mystery in which red herrings have been strung along as the story progresses. If a character hides something in Chapter Three, the chances are great that it should not be left until the end to be explained. In other words, tie up most loose ends before the climax. Don't have communal "disclose alls" after a climax, though do leave one or two matters hanging until the end.

It was not long ago that many writers had their characters hang around after the big climax scene while everything was explained. But such "tell alls" have become cliches for the most part. Few novels end this way now. Authors work harder to get explanations in before the climax, and modern readers appreciate this and expect it. To hold reader interest, however, at least one important something should be left hanging until the end — not merely an explanation but some unfinished business. If the author can delay this to the last page — even the last paragraph — reader interest is enhanced to the end.

In A Happy-Ending Story The Protagonist's Last Major Decision Is To Do Good Instead Of Bad

Abraham decides to bow to a higher authority and obey God. He agrees to sacrifice his most precious son Isaac. And instead of losing what he holds dear, he comes through the ordeal with an even stronger faith, not, of course, without suffering. The protagonist must pay some price as he proceeds to do the right thing. The price is that he suffers as he makes the morally correct choice. But because he made the right choice, he is spared the destruction that most assuredly would have engulfed him had his decision been otherwise. Despite his suffering he triumphs in the end.

Instead of a happy ending a tragic ending is assured if the protagonist chooses evil instead of good. He may gain the huge prize he desired, in Abraham's case the life of his son, but in the process he loses his soul or his life. In Faust the protagonist sells his soul to the devil, and though he lives a long and prosperous life he is condemned to eternity in hell. In the *Eye Of The Needle* the protagonist chooses to kill the woman he loved, or at least made love to, and instead he is killed. The spy also suffered greatly before losing his life.

There are some stories in which the protagonist makes the right choice and gains the prize he has been struggling for, but his decision costs him his life. This is the classic tragedy in literature, popularized by the Greeks and perfected down the centuries.

The Protagonist Must Change By The Time The Story Is Finished

Regardless of the story, short story or long, the protagonist should change dramatically. If he was arrogant, he should become compassionate; if evil, he should become good; if loving, he should become obedient (of course, unless a tragedy). The heart of every story is this change that overwhelms the protagonist. If you tell a story in which the protagonist is the same person at the start and end of your story, your reader probably will change to another story. Find the spot where a crucial emotional, moral change racked your protagonist. Then you know that your story, in that regard at least, has staying power.

The Resolution Of A Story Solves The Basic Problem That Appears At A Story's Beginning

If a girl is tied to a railroad track at the start of a story, at the end she is untied, unless it's a tragedy. Meanwhile, the story describes the origin and solution of various secondary problems.

A Good Story Ending Is Like The Ending Of A Good Joke

The best stories end with a punch that surprises and pleases.

TESTING YOUR STORY TO MAKE SURE IT'S STRONG

Nine Rules To Keep In Mind As You Finish Your Story

1. Tie up most loose ends before the climax.

2. Don't have communal "disclose alls" after climax, though do leave something hanging until the end.

3. Remember to stop when you're through. Don't add paragraph upon paragraph after you've already given all the answers.

4. Your climax is your hero's big test.

5. Don't short-change your readers in the climax. Let your reader savor your climax to the full.

6. After completing your story, check back over your dialogue and see if you have mentioned any speaker's emotion. Any such mention that involves an -ly adverb is doubly suspect (sarcastically, suspiciously, angrily, good-humoredly). Probably you can't lose them all, but certainly many of them.

7. Check back over your manuscript for any description of a speaker's actions. Try to do away with any that are physically impossible (he growled, he sneered, he grunted).

8. See if you find any words that replaced said and, if so, ask yourself if they really help. If you substituted words such as "retorted" or "answered" or "declared" or "rejoindered," do you think they call attention to themselves unnecessarily? Would it be better to return the emphasis to the dialogue?

9, See if you can get rid of some of your speaker identifications. Omit them and see if it still is clear who is speaking. Perhaps you can replace a speaker identification with a character movement.

REASONS WHY SOME MANUSCRIPTS ARE REJECTED

1. The opening is too slow.
2. The opening lacks a crucial situation.
3. Unsympathetic characters.
4. Unbelievable characters.
5. A character other than protagonist tends to steal center stage.
6. Poor contrast between characters.
7. Poor reader identification with characters.
8. Unbelievable dialogue.
9. Dialogue lacks sparkle.
10. Disproportionate mix of dialogue, action, summary.
11. Too much or too little setting.
12. Setting has been overused.
13. Plot is too familiar.
14. Not enough or too many subplots.
15. Plot moves too slowly or too quickly.
16. Scenes too hurried and short or too long.
17. Not enough scenes per chapter.
18. Author is using manuscript for a personal agenda.

Questions To Ask Before Releasing Your Manuscript

Before leaving the manuscript, let's ask ourselves the following:

1. How often did I summarize?

2. Did the main events in this plot occur in summary or in scenes?

3. If too much summary, which summarizations can be converted into scenes?

4. Have I described my character's feelings when I didn't need to? Have I *said* that my characters are generous, sad, jubilant, repentant, angry, fearful, courageous, or ambitious? Have I mentioned an emotion by name? If so, isn't it likely that I've summarized when I should have elaborated?

5. Are any of my scenes superfluous? Then away with them.

6. Did the scenes accomplish, clearly and succinctly, what I intended them to accomplish?

Another Approach To Reading A Story Aloud

Perhaps there is a friend with whom we can read the story aloud, the two of us taking different roles. In this case, when we find ourselves tempted to change some wording, there probably is a reason for such an urge.

Criticism

We are our own best critics. The longer we authors write, the clearer it becomes that we know what is best for our story. Only we really know what we're trying to say. So let's develop the ability to succeed in saying what we intended.

Also, developing the ability to become our own best editor gives us the self-confidence to screen other peoples' criticism of our work.

One of the greatest boosts toward improving an author's ability to be his own best editor is to read, perhaps as much as he writes, focusing on all kinds of literature and in particular the kind of literature that he's most interested in writing. Maybe, unknowingly, reading other peoples' work gives the author a reader's consciousness for evaluating his own.

Computer Programs That Purport To Improve Our Grammar

Computer programs intended to help an author improve grammar are only marginally successful. Typically these programs will use words such as the following to explain why they marked something in your text: capitalization, cliche, incomplete sentence, informal or colloquial, jargon, long-winded or wordy, missing comma, negative sentence, noun and verb mismatch, passive voice, possessive use incorrect, questionable usage, quotation marks, redundant, slang, split infinitive, unnecessary comma, use simpler term, use simpler word.

A canvas of several authors who have such computer programs revealed, perhaps unsurprisingly, that they prefer their own grammar judgment to that of Big Brother. Some authors have mentioned a grammar program evaluation that took the Gettysburg Address to considerable task.

Two Computer Programs To Improve Fiction Writing Are Successful

Write Pro and *Fiction Master*, two computer programs produced by Sol Stein, can help fiction writers. Even the word-processing newcomer, on the back row, far right, can probably follow Stein's relatively simple computer program instructions. Stein definitely is on target for newcomers as well as more advanced writers willing to spend extra hours or days bouncing their writing efforts against a program's fiction know-how. These are skillfully produced teaching programs that cost about as much as a half-dozen writing books but cost maybe only one-sixth the tab for a correspondence writing course. Both computer programs are included in this book's bibliography.

CALLING REVIEWERS

Many Choices

1. Have an agent or editor or publisher review it. (This one can either begin or end the list.)

2. Review it ourselves.

3. Have another writer or a non-writer friend review it.

4. Read it all or in part in a writing-course classroom.

5. Read it all or in part in a workshop or writers' club.

6.   Participate in a correspondence school for writers.

7. Employ a critiquer for hire as advertised.

8. Participate in a Writers Exchange.

SOME OF THE MORE
POPULAR CHOICES

Have An Agent Or Editor Or Publisher Review It

The chances of this happening, however, for an estimated ninety-nine percent of writers, are approximately the same as a moonbeam returning the moon-buggy left by astronauts. Most agents or editors or publishers in a position whereby money changes hands are occupied other than reading manuscripts of strangers.

Review It Ourselves

Except in approximately one percent of cases, this has to be the best place to start. Now that we've completed our manuscript, let's cool it for a few hours or weeks. Then let's read our work aloud, to our- selves or using a recorder, unless we've been reading it aloud incrementally as we wrote. In the process we either make corrections on our recorder, typed copy, or word processor, and then repeat the process for our revisions.

This book began as scribbled notes, followed over the decades by the underlining of books and articles, the highlights then triple-spaced on legal-sized yellow notebook sheets—"Old Yellow." (Incidentally, several years ago I purchased a Gregg shorthand book and since then have managed enough words so that approximately half my longhand effort is really shorthand—maybe worth a try by some authors.) I next made a directory on the word processor and typed the highlights into the directory. I then revised a first draft and have done the same with five subsequent ones.

Except for spell-checking, I prefer to do most of the editing not on my computer screen but on my HP-3 printer output, namely triple-spaced typewriter sheets. For one thing the draft printed in twelve point is easier for me to read than is the computer screen printed in almost any point. Also, as with the yellow notebook, it is easier to lug around sheets of typewriter paper than a word processor. There may be advantages to lap-tops or miniature portable keyboards, but so far they've escaped me. We can, how- ever, easily become sold on voice-operated keyboards when their efficiency goes up and the price comes down to—say—something less than a thousand or thereabouts.

Have Another Writer Or A Non-Writer Friend Review It

Ideally, a retired senior editor from a large publishing house—perchance a frustrated author himself or herself— would like to pick up some change and is available to do some reviewing at a reasonable price (that is if the retired senior editor has not been so long retired as to lose his or her publishing contacts). But, regardless, it's been my experience that spending $500 to $50,000, let's say, for an invisible product is money that might be better spent toward advertising a book once it is published. At least you can see your ad in advance.

So unless one knows, or knows of, an appropriate professional critiquer, I would suggest using a friend who is more than friendly. After all, what are friends—or friendly people—for? A spouse is a good person with whom to start. Or let's hope so. Or another friend. Or a neighbor. Or a fellow-writer in a Writer's Exchange program.

I have found it helpful to show the reviewer the following list of points to consider:

REVIEW CHECKPOINTS

(1) Characters
(2) Plot
(3) Prose
(4) Setting
(5) Subject matter
(6) Inconsistencies
(7) Highlights
(8) Length
(9) Title
(10) Originality

Critiquer Rapport

If the reader is not that close a friend, or has already read more than his or her share of your manuscripts, a $100 or thereabouts "coffee fund" check accompanying your manuscript could be considered a polite introduction.

Pseudonyms, used by various writers, can be of help in depersonalizing your relationship with a critiquer. The S. C. Lee (Stonewall Culpepper Lee) pseudonym has made it easier for some of my readers to be carnivorously blunt. This works even if this sobriquet is a very thin veil between you and your critiquer.

Regardless, remind your critiquers to be sure and say what they think. If the majority denigrate the same critique items, you should know what areas need help.

STORYTELLING

You might try telling your story "voco" to someone rather than handing that someone a copy of your manuscript. It could be that what you leave out in telling your story means something. It could mean that what you omitted orally should be omitted from your manuscript.

Rewriting Your Manuscript

Again, you can become your own best critic. After your manuscript "cools," whatever in it strikes you as bad quite likely is. Polishing your manuscript may hurt you--some have equated it with throwing babies into a fire--but at least it's not the readers' babies.

What About Attending Writing Courses?

Having your manuscript critiqued in a writing-course classroom can be time-consuming. You will be sharing your time with fellow class members. The instructor's advice concerning other manuscripts may or may not apply to your work. You may even find the critiques of your teacher and your students unhelpful when directed at your own manuscript. Typically, the more untalented a writer, the more criticizing time is required in a group. This is not to underestimate the obvious advantages of attending writing courses. When you attend class, as occurs when you attend church, typically you meet kindred spirits. Such friendships appear to be even more enduring than those from sororities or fraternities, for example. Writing relationships often expand after completion of a course. But, again, such classes are time-consuming. If a story bores you, you can't skip ten pages in a class as you can in a book. Which obviously is a back door way to introduce this plug: reading books about writing may well be the best way to learn more about writing.

Read It All Or In Part In A Workshop Or Writers' Club

Some of the concerns regarding writing classes also apply to writing organizations and workshops. What you find yourself exposed to may not apply to your needs. Attending meetings may not be as convenient as reading about writing. There may not even be meetings available to you. On the plus side, participation in writing organizations or workshops may provide contacts for you with agents, editors, or publishers.

Participate In A Correspondence School For Writers

Correspondence schools can fulfill the needs of certain authors. Because of geography or time limitations, some authors may find correspondence schools their best tutor. Others may be too timid to have their material reviewed in an open forum.

But in most cases authors will find correspondence courses a major gamble. For those with money to spare and a gambling heart, there should be no major problem. But others should start cautiously by requesting a free copy of the Directory of Accredited Home Study Schools, National Home Study Council, 1601 18th Street NW, Washington, DC 20009. Then the author should request catalogues from the schools that look most promising, and peruse the catalogues to select the best schools. Here are questions that should lead to identifying better schools:

1. Do the prices quoted in their catalogue cover all charges, including unscheduled charges downstream?

2. With whom on the faculty will you be dealing? Their credentials?

3. If not covered in the catalogue, what does the school do toward helping to sell a student's work?

4. If not covered in the catalogue, what about academic credits for a completed course?

5. If the unforeseen happens, what is the school's refund policy?

If you feel that correspondence training could mean a major dent in your time or money, you should check further before enrolling in a school. A visit with your librarian or a visit, letter, or call to your Congressman's office can help you identify agencies that evaluate correspondence schools, in particular regarding complaints. Many banks help steer customers to evaluating organizations that can help you evaluate your potential alma mater. Let's remember that it's your time, your money, and your future as a writer that's involved. Your characters deserve a careful creator.

Employ A Critiquer For Hire As Advertised

This is another area in which to remain forever wary. But, once more, if you have extra time and money and a gambling heart, you might want to respond to critiquing agencies whose advertisements you see in publications and in direct mail. For those interested, here are things to check before hiring a professional critiquer to handle your work: (1) Ask for a written statement of services and charges; (2) Get the name and address or phone number of some recent clients; (3) Get the name and address or phone number of editors who have bought their clients' work recently; (4) Consult monitoring agencies as suggested for authors checking correspondence schools.

Participate In A Writers Exchange

Further discussion of this program comes later in this book, under the heading "What About Those Twenty Million Manuscripts And More?" This writing improvement plan involves writers reviewing each others' manuscripts without charge. It's a revival example of barter payment, this one featuring swapped criticism.

Reader Reaction In A Word

As we and others review our manuscript, the most important thing to keep in mind is specific reader reaction to it. Will our readers find what we have to say boring, controversial, enlightening, repitious, interesting, nonsensical, reassuring, disturbing, innovative, confusing, threatening, informative? In other words, what specifically should be, and probably will be, their reaction to our communication? Our writing should incite our readers to the reaction we desire. We must remember the readers' interests throughout our writing.

Ending Of *Farewell To Arms* Rewritten Thirty-Nine Times

After a "cooling-off" time lasting anywhere from a few hours to days and even weeks and months, most authors revise their manuscripts and repeat the process several times. Ernest Hemingway once stated that he rewrote the ending of *Farewell To Arms* "thirty-nine times." You should count on revising your work as many as half a dozen times before you consider it complete. To make revision easier, double-space or triple-space between lines on your yellow notebook or typing paper.

Hemingway had his own way of relaxing during those "cooling off" intervals. Some critics have accused him of spending too many hours in non-literary pursuits such as hunting, or frequenting bars that are now tourist attractions in his memory. The average writer, disdaining an attack mode, simply "cools off" as a writer and then returns with a warm glow called "Reader perspective."

NO MORE RETIRING TO GARRETS

"How Not To Be Retiring"

Smooth Selling Required

Or--navigating the selling rapids.

Offer Different Versions Of Your Work

Reprint, audio, abridged, or whatever, try to sell your manuscript in various forms, always crediting the main work as you submit variations. This should improve sales of the main work.

Endorsements For Your Story

Decide what kind of endorsement would make you want to read someone else's story, and experiment with that level of endorsement for your's. Would an endorsement, say, by a household name impress you? A cabinet member in Washington? A senator? A governor? A well-known writer? An expert in your story's subject matter? Perhaps a telephone operator can furnish you a person's mailing address for a small charge. Various WHO'S WHO and other publications in the library have a surprising number of addressees of famous people or experts in your main area of interest. Explain briefly what your story is about and why this subject might be of special interest to those endorsers you seek. Offer to send them appropriate pages for their review (or a copy of the entire manuscript, if they request it). Tell them why you are seeking an endorsement. Be sure and enclose an SASE (self-addressed stamped envelope). You may be surprised at the response.

Shall We Try A Publisher Or An Agent Or Both?

The answer is yes, until we sell our story or decide to look elsewhere in this complicated journey. The process of selling a manuscript used to be much simpler. There was a time before conglomerates took over publishing, before computer printing and sales technology entered the picture. Then some efficiency experts determined that publishers should not receive unsolicited manuscripts, relying instead on agents or established clients.

So agents are now receiving the publishers' mail as well as their own. As a result, overworked agents are meeting postmen at the door, sharing water glasses and heart tablets, and commiserating concerning increased postal rates. Yes, competition is fierce. With many agents and publishers, the long-queue approach is the only real ball game in town.

However, here is the best advice for submitting your story to an agent or publisher. At your library or bookstore, locate books or magazines featuring story-selling. The best are listed in this book's bibliography and include such names as *LITERARY MARKET PLACE, WRITERS DIGEST*, *WRITERS MARKET,* and *WRITERS YEARBOOK.* Locate the name of an appropriate editor and address your inquiry by name to help garner a response and avoid the notorious "slush pile."

Probably a one-page letter is sufficient for initiating proceedings, unless an agent or publisher has stated a desire, let's say, for three chapters and an outline or the first fifty pages (or unless you feel you really can't explain your story in a page). Near the start of your letter try to mention briefly something catchy about your story, a line for example that might appear on the front of a magazine to capture impulse buyers at the checkout counter.

In addition to your letter stating your story's subject and mentioning its highlights, you can mention your writing credits, if any. These credits can include writing-course enrollment, workshops attended, or writing degrees earned, if your background is not overburdened with writing credits per se. If you wish, you can mention why your subject is timely and why it is better than or differs from its competition. Then include your SASE and be prepared to wait.

If you are lucky, you may hear something within a couple weeks or so. Either when you submit your first copy or later, you may want to do the same with another agent or publisher, informing the first that you are making multiple submissions. Many agents and publishers claim not to resent multiple submissions and may not castigate authors for "taking advantage of franking privilege." On the other hand, some agents and publishers may resent it. Regardless, there seems to be no basic difference between multiple submissions and auctioning manuscripts or books. So why not be venturesome?

Your Best Chance Of Finding A Good Agent Is *After* You Have Found A Good Publisher, Or At Least A Publisher

Since an unagented author's chances are 99 to 1 against finding an appropriate agent or publisher, what now? Well, return to the horse's mouth, as mentioned earlier, by sending letters of inquiry to agents and publishers, simultaneously working to either improve your manuscript or start another. and you might want to sprinkle in a few phone calls. Again, if you get a publishing offer from a publisher, agenting should become easier. This makes sense. At only 10-to-15 percent commission for selling a manuscript, agents can afford little time to experiment with unknowns.

The best time for an author to find an agent is when the author has an offer from a publisher but has not yet signed a contract. An agent probably would be worthwhile in negotiating your contract with a publisher. Then quite likely with your next book you will have both a publisher and an agent. Your editor at a publishing house can recommend a good agent for you. You can get information about agents from organizations such as the Society of Authors' Representatives and the Independent Literary Agents Association in New York. The addresses are in the back of this book. *THE LITERARY MARKET PLACE*, probably in the reference section in your local library, offers much information helpful to writers, including information about those two organizations and many others. Your library may also have a copy of *PUBLISHERS WEEKLY,* long an information bonanza for authors as well as agents, publishers, and book sellers.

Contacts

Selling a manuscript is like selling a car or almost anything in a highly competitive market. If buyers don't come to you, and of course too often they don't, then go where the action is. With a car, once your classified ads don't work, this can mean renting space at a car sales lot or taking your car to a car auction. With a manuscript or manuscript idea you can begin making contacts with professional writers and agents and editors, often on weekends, attending one or more of the hundreds of conferences and workshops held each year. Your primary goal now is to sell instead of learning to write better. Professional writers, agents, editors, and publishers' representatives are often more approachable at this time. A bonus for many would be to discover an outstanding manuscript. Even if a writer isn't fortunate enough to make a worthwhile contact with one of the above, perhaps the writer can meet one or more fellow writers who make contacts and then remember to extend a hand down the ladder.

The Importance Of Contacts

The importance of meeting the right people, even more so than when selling a car, cannot be overestimated in publishing. If the primary target is missed, perhaps someone knows the spouse, or a friend of the spouse. Perhaps a cousin or niece or nephew knows someone. Maybe there is word of a position just opened in a publishing house. If you are not interested, some of your relatives right out of college could be. Long shots, certainly, but still on the range. And of course what ultimately counts is a manuscript's merit more than its author's contacts. But, by definition, luck hath no weight limit. Or, as Will Rogers said, and quoted previously, "The harder I work the luckier I get."

Subject Guide To Books In Print A Good Tool

This multi-volumed directory, listing about 800,000 books, is an excellent reference for an author when selling a story as well as when selecting a subject. If a publisher carries several titles in your subject area, he's at least as likely to want more as he is to feel overloaded.

Manuscript Security

We don't want to become so engrossed in attempting to sell our manuscript that we forget to keep a copy.

Again, Think Of A Label Or A Slogan That Will Help Merchandise Your Manuscript

Visualize someone introducing you or your story to an audience. What choice phrase would you want them to use? Or perhaps you've written a story for a magazine, and you visualize a few apt words on a magazine's cover, based on your story and intended to entice impulse buyers. In the case of this book about writing, the first words that came to mind were "Senior Write-Right Advisor," later determined to be flippant and unclear and changed to read "Senior Writing Advisor," hopefully an improvement.

An Author Is Ultimately Responsible No Matter Who Publishes His Story

An author has certain major responsibilities for his story, no matter if someone else publishes it or he publishes it himself. The author makes suggestions as to where some of the 50 to 500 review copies should go, though often this is guesswork at best. Sometimes the nebulous names and addresses and strictures of book reviewers leave the author feeling like a handcuffed pushup expert attempting to throw darts in the dark. But in general, three months in advance of your book's publication, someone on your side should send galleys — not bound books—to the *NEW YORK TIMES BOOK REVIEW, PUBLISHERS WEEKLY, LIBRARY JOURNAL, SCHOOL LIBRARY JOURNAL* as appropriate, *BOOKLIST,*

KIRKUS REVIEWS, and other monthlies that review books before or near date of publication.

After bound copies are available, bound books should be sent to book review editors at large newspapers such as the *WASHINGTON POST, LOS ANGELES TIMES,* and the *CHICAGO TRIBUNE* as well as other appropriate publications.

Make Your Computer Disk Available To Editors And Publishers

If you have used a word processor in writing your story, your investment can save some editors and publishers time and money, if they choose to take advantage of it.

An Ideal Way To Design Your Work For Easy Printing

Select one or more printed books or periodicals that you would like to use as a model. Measure its page size, line length, distance between lines, and margin for text and headers and page numbers. Experiment until you have matched the font style and size that you like. Use of a role model is helpful whether we prepare our own camera-ready copy, or forward our story to a printer or publisher who will prepare the camera-ready (copy ready to be photographed for printing). It may help to refer both the printer and the publisher to the role-model book or books you have in mind.

YOUR BEST BET FOR A PRINTING FIRM

"The Future Is Now"

Imagine a country where authors are knighted as kings and queens. Where those less lucky are publishers, agents, or book sellers. Today anyone with spare cash can be a publisher promptly. Printing On Demand (POD) and Electronic Printing (EP) assure it. Eager readers demand it. And more, for a few hundred dollars we don't even need a keyboard. We simply talk to our computer as to any servent awaiting our command. The computer then taps the keyboard for us--we don't even have to do that.

Let's recapitulate what we know about publishing and perhaps throw a little more light onto those intriguing buzz words in today's publishing world: Traditional Printing, Printing On Demand, and Electronic Printing. The astute reader may find some duplication in the following few pages, and indeed there is, making it perfectly permissible to skip to the next section. But for those interested in this moment's perspective of publishing vernaculers, the following few paragraphs if not pages are personally yours.

Just a few months ago there were nervous debates concerning which way to publish: Traditional, POD, or EP. Today most votes are in. The foremost factor in print selection seems to be how many copies of a publication we desire. If we have in mind reaching thousands on this first run, we consider Traditional Printing or Electronic Printing. If limited to the hundreds, we're prime candidates for Printing On Demand.

PRINTING BY ANY OTHER NAME

This may be the place to mention briefly another new printing term, Print Quantity Needed (PQN). The term seems somewhat questionable, maybe even on the confusion side of the alphabet. As we know, all publishers print quantities we consider needed. So let's not include the category in this exercise. Our workout is sufficiently strenuous as it is.

CHOOSING TRADITIONAL OR DEMAND OR ELECTRONIC

How does one handle all this confusion about which technology to use in printing a book or article? Well, certain guidelines apply. First the author should maintain as much control as possible in the publishing process. Release the publishing responsibility only as far as you, not someone else, decide. Try not to let someone else give your publication a cradle-to-grave approach. Lest grave prove the keyword.

Selection of traditional, demand, electronic printing usually comes back to number of copies desired. Five hundred copies seems to be a favorite number for deciding between demand and traditional, with traditional claiming big numbers. Print quantity is less crucial in deciding to go electronic. Certainly much less preparation is required in flashing a manuscript onto a screen rather than binding it for readers to have and to hold.

A major problem in all this is of course human ego. How many of us would fool with a manuscript to start with if we thought only a few readers would participate? We're probably less confident about selling and distributing techniques than in our manuscript itself. You may have started with the question, "Did I ever tell you about Uncle George and the loose bear?" Certainly this is of interest to more than cousin Gertrude.

There's nothing wrong with POD or EP. But don't flaunt the former against a wide range of traditional publication-reviewers. And don't feature EP among the elderly or people of poor eyesight.

For the gambling author with, let's say, a thousand or two extra dollars, traditional printing with an initial run of 2,000 or 3,000 copies might be most appropriate. For the average author, it probably is cheaper and otherwise more gratifying to try POD. For authors desiring to test the new technological frontier, EP may be it.

Traditional Printing

More than 90% of books printed annually in the U. S. are printed the traditional, old-fashioned way. In traditional printing, a camera makes a picture of everything on a sheet of paper, the picture is transferred to a printing plate, and after such "pre press" the plate is slapped onto the press, the press is oiled with printer's ink, and out comes the book ready for binding.

Following are sample price lists for printing books the old-fashioned, traditional way. The first firm is quoting cheaper than the second primarily because it is quoting cheaper paper. White offset 50# is thinner than white offset 60#, and 512 ppi (pages per inch) is thinner than 392 ppi. Shorter books sometimes have bulkier paper in order to look longer. It typically is best to get several quotes before committing to any printer.

SAMPLE TRADITIONAL PRICE LIST

QUANTITY: 100, 500, 3,000
TRIM: 6 X 9
PAGES: 200
TEXT: Camera-ready copy or files. Black ink.
COVER: 4-color process. Laminated.
STOCK: 50# white offset, 512 ppi, 10 pt.
cover.   4-color. Process. Laminated.
BINDING: Perfect binding in 32s.
PACKING: 56 books per carton.
SHIPPING: FOB printer.
PRICE: 100 copies = $2,418; 500 copies = $2, 769; 3,000 copies = $4,984.00

ANOTHER SAMPLE TRADITIONAL PRICE LIST

QUANTITY: 1,000, 1500, 3000
TRIM: 6 x 9
PAGES: 200
TEXT: Printing black throughout.
COVER: 4-color process, laminated.
STOCK: 60# white offset. 392 (average) ppi
BINDING: Adhesive paper cover.
PACKING: Bulk pack.
SHIPPING: FOB printer.
PRICE: 1,000 = $3469; 1,500 = $4024; 3,000 = $5662

We're estimating that if we'd selected only a 1,000 run, the price per copy would be around $2.75 each compared to a 3,000 selection at $2.00 each or compared to 5,000 copies at $1.50 each. These prices do not include pre-press costs such as typesetting and editing, which will be the same regardless of kind or quantity of printing.

So much for printing cost for the moment. How can we get back our investment and make a modest profit, though probably never enough to pay for all the labor and even love already put into our project. Well, the publisher's rule of thumb for recovering publishing costs and earning that modest profit is to price our publication at eight to ten times production cost. So if our 3,000 copies cost about $2.00 each, the price on the publication itself should be at least eight times that or around $16.95. True, wholesalers, distributors, bookstores, sales reps, and inventories are still needed under this scenario, but wait.

POD is probably faster and costs less overall. If Print On Demand produces a few copies of a book that sells well, it can be printed in larger quantities the old-fashioned way. Or at any point it can be published electronically for reading on a screen. Or audio for pleasant listening to one or more speakers. Meanwhile, as for readers, they share the best of two worlds. They can hold the author's work in their hands, or talk to the author over live computer, or can read the author's work simply by adjusting the Lazy Boy and glancing toward the screen. They need not worry whether or not a book is Traditional, POD, or EP.

PRINTING ON DEMAND

At present, state of the art POD is less geared for mass production than is traditional printing, and so POD normally is relegated to short runs. Short runs of less than, say, five hundred copies should be candidates for POD.

Printing On Demand could help solve the perennial problem of book returns. It should minimize if not end the need for distributors, and it definitely will end the tendency for a long lapse in time between receipt of a manuscript and printing it. It will inspire reprints of many out-of-print or almost out-of-print books and can make a few copies available almost with the touch of a button.

Following is a sample POD price list giving cost per book for sample book size and number of pages:

SAMPLE PRINTING ON DEMAND PRICE LIST

SIZE =	5.5 X 8.5	6 x 9	8.5 x 11
200 = PAGES	$3.42	$4.22	$4.82
300 = PAGES	$4.07	$5.32	$5.83

MINIMUM ORDER 50 COPIES; ONE-TIME SET-UP FEE, $50.00; TO 700 PAGES.

Prices are changing so rapidly in the Printing On Demand arena, these figures are fleeting. Regardless, the average author can expect to pay considerably more than an originally cited price. Roughly, with EP as well as POD, the author should maybe expect to pay double the original price quotes, once the various options, services, discounts, and royalties are revealed and tallied.

The preceding price list seems the way to go for those who prefer to invest a few hundred dollars POD as opposed to several thousand for traditional printing. POD typically requires less investment for getting a few hundred copies of a book, and Traditional Printing requires less per book for longer runs.

Let's assume that we immediately need several hundred copies of our book for whatever reason, which brings POD to the forefront. Perhaps the subject of our biography just died, or an emerging bank has requested a hundred premium copies for opening day, or we have just learned of a distant and to us impromptu family reunion.

Time is on our side but cost may not be. POD has the price markup of the newly invented. POD printers have a major investment in their equipment. Even a small print shop needs a $50,000 or so investment just to crank up, and it must still print with considerable "hands on." A Xerox Docutech demands a $250,000 price plus cost of options. IBM and Oce' use fully-automated POD equipment so that what goes in one end comes out a published product--with little if any "hands on" required. But these Print On Demand systems cost approximately a million dollars. Some traditional printers have added POD services, some copy shops are expanding into this, and many digital printing firms have begun business and are eagerly awaiting customers. But in the arena of digital printing, so far there is little loose money in the game.

Publishing 50 or 100 copies POD might cost $5.00 a copy, not including pre-publication costs. But the book will bring in around $7.95 ($16.95 less 50% discount on the average). And so here at our fingertips we have the future now. No need for agents, publishers, wholesalers, distributors, bookstores, warehouses, to get our manuscript published and moving. No need to be swamped with bookstore returns. Who needs to store large inventories rather than orders? Books need never go out of print. We have our manuscript published, with millions of potential customer out there on the Net.

ELECTRONIC PRINTING

But now this. Also here is EP enhanced by technological developments such as flexible electronic displays. Electronic paper, first developed by Xerox Parc in the 1970s, features improvements now being developed by E Ink and by the Xerox offshoot company Gyricon Media. Other developments are Organic Light-Emitting Diode (OLED) displays, developed by Kodak in the 1980s, with Kodak continuing to pioneer additional development. Though major improvements of electronic paper OLEDs and LEPs may take three or four more years of development, and it may take two or three additional years before an even more satisfying reading experience develops, Electronic Publishing is already challenging Traditional and Print On Demand systems for mankind's literary communication future.

In the future many readers will read primarily from screens or so-called monitors rather than from books printed with type. Stephen King's book *Riding The Bullet* proved to be the fastest selling book of all time thanks to electronic publishing, namely displaying his book on computer screens. Fastest, that is, if we can call it sales when many of the first day's 400,000 copies were distributed free, and if we call a downloadable but not printable electronic text a book. Regardless, these customers were content to receive the material on their computer screen rather than as a book as in the past.

With Publishing On Demand and Electronic Publishing, the author can publish a full-sized (say 200 or 300-page) book within several days the first publishing and within hours the next. Regardless of those earlier somber predictions about "Web Selling," the astute author has learned that selling on the Web is learnable, in fact as easy as taking candy from a baby, except in this case giving candy to a baby. As a teaser, the potential customer is given something, perhaps a free chapter from a book, or the first page of each chapter, or a summary of Siam's annual rainfall, in return for which money, it is hoped, eventually changes hands.

WE'VE ENTERED OUR HARBOR BUT ARE WE READY?

Let It Cool

Perhaps we can have a friend or acquaintance read it and make suggestions, including editing. Various successful authors pay people in their own town to read and critique their manuscript, often for say a hundred or so dollars. The results reportedly have been good. After all, one doesn't need to be in publishing to read and react to a manuscript or book.

Word Doctors

So now we're reminded of retired book editors (book doctors) in New York and elsewhere. PUBLISHERS WEEKLY magazine had an interesting article containing a couple of photos of New York "word doctors." Their charges are as much as $1,000 or more per manuscript, but even if an author spends this, the time factor can be a real problem. One 450-page manuscript went to a New York word doctor only to have the author four months later receive it back with an explanation that the editor couldn't handle it because of family problems. The reading fee would have been approximately $1,000. Another retired editor "word doctor" told that author that this editing fee was vastly too low to start with, probably contributing to the delay. But for those who would rather have a better book than a trip, say, to Disneyland, a thousand dollars to a word doctor could help assure lasting returns.

Changing Minds At Blue-Lines Stage

After a final polish of our manuscript, we start looking, warily to be sure, at what more we can do to our manuscript locally before sending it to a printer. Printers sometimes employ creative accounting when it comes to charging for something the author could or should have done. For example, misspelled words should be corrected long before the manuscript goes to the printer. The so-called "blue-line" stage, normally the last proof before printing the book, should come far too late for such revisions. Instead let's try to minimize blue-line corrections lest the color blue suggest the customer as well as the proof.

Quantity Considerations

Money can help an author leap over many a hurdle, but lack of money can solve many a problem also. An author needs little money if he only wants a book for himself and a few friends. No word doctors. No paid editors. No professional critiquers. No writing classes. No seminars. A few hundred dollars for Printing

On Demand is sufficient for a few copies for the author and friends. But if we think of larger distribution, even a bestseller, and have that gambling spirit and a few thousand dollars, printing our document the old-fashioned "ink on paper" way probably is most appropriate, for now at least.

The chances of an author finding someone else to pay for publishing his manuscript are almost nil. Almost all publishers now require that a manuscript be filtered through an agent before they'll consider it, a marriage not necessarily made in Heaven. The average rejection rate for manuscripts submitted to literary agents has been cited as 98%. This is flooding the top agents, with 500,000 manuscripts reportedly written in the U. S. each year. It's estimated that less than 50,000 are published, so someone had to do some rejecting. Countless authors have vivid memories of going in the front door of an agent's office and seeing the agent fleeing out back. Meanwhile the authors have not even seen the domains of editors or publishers.

Printing Guidelines

This returns us full-fledged to printing our manuscript ourselves, either traditionally, or on demand, or so-called electronically. Ideally, we can send the printer our manuscript on a disk, or, less desirably, send it as camera ready copy. We can also send the manuscript for the printer himself to typeset. Generally, in this typesetting stage, corrections should be minimized. This is an important point, especially if we remember that a typeset page can look drastically different from a manuscript's.

Request For Quotation

Ordinarily it's a good idea to get quotes from at least a half-dozen printers experienced with books before releasing a book for printing. Author associations, author-publishers, and manuals about publishing can often help with names and addresses of such printers.

Following is the form that we used in obtaining quotes for this book you are reading. If you wish you may make copies of this form and mail them to printers. You'll note that one request is a quote for printing 5,000 copies. Of course, we in our case actually requested quotes for printing an estimated several hundred thousand for our initial first run but were too modest to mention it here.

The CIS in the cover specification stands for Coated One Side. The PPI relative to paper specification stands for Pages Per Inch. Both are explained in more detail in this book's glossary.

Recommended Form

REQUEST FOR QUOTATION

Please quote your best price for printing and binding the following book. You will receive it as a Portable Document Format (or whatever) file.

TITLE OF BOOK: HOW TO WRITE AND GET IT PUBLISHED

AUTHOR: DAVID AKENS

QUANTITY: 2,000. 3000. 5000

NUMBER OF PAGES: 240

TRIM SIZE: 6 X 9

ILLUSTRATIONS: NONE

COVER: PUBLISHER SUPPLIES MATERIAL FOR PRINTER TO PRINT 4-COLOR COVER, FRONT, SPINE, AND BACK. 12 POINT CIS LAMINATED

PAPER TEXT: 60 POUND WHITE OFFSET (HIGH BULK LOW PPI)

TEXT: BLACK THROUGHOUT

PROOFS: COMPLETE BLUELINES

BINDING: PERFECT

PACKAGING: CARTONS SHALL WEIGH NO MORE THAN 30 POUNDS

TERMS: ONE THIRD DOWN, ONE THIRD WITH ACCEPTANCE OF BLUE LINES, AND ONE THIRD WITHIN 30 DAYS OF RECEIPT OF BOOKS.
CREDIT REFERENCES IF DESIRED.

DEADLINE: PLEASE QUOTE BY
_____

YOUR QUOTE:

OVERRUNS:

REPRINT OF 3,000

REPRINT OF 5,000

DELIVERY CHARGES: PRICES INCLUDE DELIVERY OF BOOKS TO PUBLISHER

DISCOUNT FOR PROMPT PAYMENT:

ESTIMATED DELIVERY TIME:

MISCELLANEOUS CHARGES:

PRINTER REMARKS:

SIGNED:

PRINTER NAME:

DATE:

ANYTHING ELSE, OTHER THAN PROMPT PAYMENT, THAT MIGHT RESULT IN LOWER PRICE TO PUBLISHER:

IT IS AGREED THAT ALL MATERIAL FURNISHED BY THE PUBLISHER SHALL BE RETURNED TO THE PUBLISHER UPON COMPLETION OF THE PRINTING AND BINDING BY PRINTER.

First Book Authors Can Do Almost All

At least with a first book, an author should do much of the work, or fun, as the author perceives it. With this book you are reading the author did everything except rotate the printing presses.

Sales In The Sunset

Let's assume that we want to sell more than one copy of our book. We've decided that by cutting corners we can manage to publish a hundred copies, most likely by Printing On Demand. Let's turn those one hundred into review copies, for some reason a magic minimum review number at most serious publishers. We mail these copies along with a news release about our book to review outlets as listed in publications such as *Literary Market Place* or *Publishers' Trade List Annual* (see bibliography), including a book review editor at major newspapers (simply addressed to Book Review Editor).

Include among your book reviewers book buyers for major bookstore chains or distributors, including wholesalers. Judith Appelbaum's *How To Get Happily Published* (in her section called "Resources") has an outstanding list of people and firms to contact.

All this of course can result in only one of two responses, either Good News or Bad News. If good news, with enough reviewers reviewing your work favorably, don't worry, you'll know it. Book buyers will make their wonderful presence known at your doorstep. If they don't, then you can proceed with the bad news approach, which you should have started with anyway if you could. You prepare a pamphlet (flyer) describing your book and test the market by mailing a couple hundred to names you can rent from firms that writing magazines will list or your local librarian can help you find. If the response is as much as 2% or 3%, then you can consider proceeding with a mass mailing to similar recipients. If the response is less than that, then forget that arena and perhaps try a small cheap ad somewhere and stay prepared for bad results because everyone else is doing the same. Still, it might be different with us.

On a limited scale, limited by your time, autographings can account for some sales at specific locations, and enough of those on a wide enough canvas can at least help defray publishing expenses. Talk shows are an increasingly popular medium for free author and book exposure, but unless someone *is* someone, or has done something such as parachuting off Mount Everest, the postman may never bring an appropriately addressed invitation.

The best way to entice readers, short of spectacular news releases, is to offer the reader something free. Assuming that we do not want to promise the reader a hundred dollars for every typo, a gift of part of our opus sometimes works. Author King, mentioned earlier, gave away some of his novel on the Internet to interest readers. Perhaps the author can think of a subject that will interest readers, and furnish this information free on the Internet or off, with an afterthought concerning the work that *is* for sale.

In general, authors should realize that writing well is only half the battle. The other half, and certainly as important, is selling not only well but spectacularly. Yes, we can't have one half without the other, or at least don't want to. That is why Presidents Jimmy Carter and Bill Clinton and the others are on talk shows, touting their writing and explaining how they came through every hardship to all this.

Printers Who Sell Books

Once more, be wary of those who claim they can help you sell what they print. Apples and oranges. Man cannot serve two masters. Normally, good printers do not claim to be good publishers, as in selling as well as printing. Publishers might claim to be good printers if they have their own printing department. But an author's book jacket flashed on a screen with hundreds of others will serve largely for comparing jackets instead of money changing hands.

Publish Or Perish

On university campuses especially, professors are aware of the axiom "Publish Or Perish." But what if a person has only one publication in mind without thought of becoming a publisher? As this book went to press, a review copy of a book arrived along with a letter from the head of a national education foundation, a former university president. Other than this one book he indicates no desire to become a publisher. Presumably he has the $500 or so to print a Print On Demand book and life will unfold joyfully ever after.

The following axioms, that indeed guided our reply to this author, are meant to apply to any author, from rich to barely solvent, foundation head or no foundation head. By the way, this educator-author has done a very wise thing. At the top of his book's front cover, in about 16-point type, he has these words: DRAFT: REVIEW COPY. Such words give his book prestige, a review copy no end.

1. Some reviewers demand books at least three months in advance of publication, calling for advance copies such as this one. For all we know this may be an advance review copy from a million-copy run and the author is playing the advance-copy game exactly right.

2. Perhaps there are mistakes, glaring or otherwise, in the book. What better way to catch them before the million-copy run? In this case the publisher, in the eyes of the reviewer, is less meaningful. Even if it is an unassuming author he's had enough faith in his manuscript to change a manuscript to a bound copy and distribute it. Regardless of what anyone says or thinks,

here's one author at least who certainly has published at least one book.

In essence, receipt of the educator's review copy reminded us that no matter how successful the author is otherwise, the wise one will follow basic selling guidelines.

Bound To Win

We've been going to press for a number of pages, mainly between clips at the barber shop, and our barber's advice is to do something, even if it's wrong. The barber inquired pointedly about book publishing progress and then pointed out that it's no problem to write a book "but try selling it."

Inspired by this hint of wisdom I left the shop determined to name my own thought for the day. Let's call it Edort Publishing's basic rule for success. Any venturesome author should first take his manuscript to the nearest quick copy emporium and have about a half dozen copies run off and "shop bound." The copies can go to readers with review or at least reaction potential.

Based upon reaction to these few copies the author will or won't print a hundred or so Print On Demand copies. Based on reaction to a hundred or so Print On Demand copies we do or don't print several thousand copies the Traditional way.

So, in this innovative technologicl era one approach to systematic publishing can be the following three steps:

1.   If you want to proceed with your eyes open and your billfold intact, quick-copy a half dozen copies of your book for review or at least reaction.

2. Based upon positive reaction, print a hundred or so test copies for sale.

3. If we are still moving forward, Print On Demand hundreds more, or thousands more the Traditional way.

Obviously, the preceding is for those authors who like to wade before they dive.

SELLING PUBLISHED BOOK OR ARTICLE

The Options Are Limitless

In this new technological age, bursting with communication innovations, variation in publishing is momentous. Near the midst of everything is book publishing, and important in this is rapidly increased self-publishing. In fact, today may be known as the Age of Self Publishing with computers as our tools.

General acceptance is overcoming the reluctance, perhaps even innate timidity, some authors have when it comes to extolling the virtues of their own work. In this age of speed, more and more authors are declining to accept the one or two years used for publishing most books, especially when Printing On Demand and certainly Electronic Printing offer such relatively economical and rapid publishing. The now increasing number of self-publishers is lofting a new banner over the publishing arena.

In line with all this, as more and more self-published books succeed, respectful attitudes toward self-publishing are increasingly evident among book reviewers and librarians and readers as well as the public. Furthermore, self-publishing simplifies the whole publishing process, as the only person the author needs to please is himself and potential readers. This chapter describes some aspects of self-publishing in selling publications.

Local Contacts

In addition to arranging for a reading at a local library or bookstore, the author should arrange for autographings, meanwhile autographing all the store's copies of the book because autographed copies are more likely to sell. The author should also contact the local newspaper, magazine, radio, and television stations to inform them that a local author has authored a published book. Because juggling money can be awkward at personal appearances, some authors take a friend along to transact sales.

Radio Or Television Or Computer

Make a list of provocative questions that an interviewer might ask, and then practice answering them fast and fully. Since the average interview on radio or television lasts a half dozen minutes or more (and probably longer on computers), there's time to establish empathy with your potential buyers as you mention your book with considered frequency. All you need for preparation are a few rehearsals.

Sales Ingenuity

One of New York's leading literary agencies or agent responds to thousands of inquiries from aspiring authors by sending authors its own sales pitch along with the apparently mandatory rejection slip. The sales pitch, of rejection slip size, is a fragment of paper explaining that one of the respected members has written a book about writing. A free chapter can be viewed at the agency's home page address on the Internet.

This is not to question such a tactic. In this case, though, the book's title suggests that the agent-author is here to help the frantic ninety-nine percent of authors rejected by agents, but the free Internet tidbits contain much more information about the book's format than helpful suggestions about writing and selling.

This example of sales ingenuity points to its widespread application.

The Difference Between Your Book And Its Competitors

Some of the most important messages in book sales are those contrasting the difference between your book and its competition. These crucial messages can be used with book covers, news releases, media advertising, direct-mail flyers or pamphlets, and — among other things — a sales rep's ticket to book buyers, as well as letters of inquiry.

Almost All Authors Should Be A Super Seller Or Wealthy Or Famous

These days, writing the story is rarely enough. If a book is competently written, nothing sells a book better than the author's on-stage selling ability.

Ways To Advertise A Book

Far too often a display ad in a newspaper or magazine does not pay (this does not include classified advertising or a display ad advertising a special event such as an autographing). Large, uneconomical display ads, sometimes used to make the author feel good, can cost from a few dollars in small newspapers to the area of $20,000 for a full page ad in the *NEW YORK TIMES* Book Review section. Probably the best way to advertise a book, apart from advertising an author presentation such as an autographing or library reading, is through direct mail advertising to a group with special interest in the book's subject (for example farmers if the book is about wheat combines) or through advertising the same book in specialized media, (such as, for example, the *PROGRESSIVE FARMER).* Regardless of the merchandising approach, however, the most effective and least costly way to sell a book remains word-of-mouth and book reviews.

Is Your Work Being Copyrighted?

Before proceeding into the selling mode, why not reassure yourself concerning your story's copyright status? Under the 1976 Copyright Act, which became effective January 1, 1978, "a work of original authorship is protected by copyright from the time the work is created in fixed form." But though your work is protected by copyright when you complete it, in some cases such as litigation there can be advantages in having your copyright placed on public record at the Copyright Office at the Library of Congress in Washington. It might be a good idea to send a copy of your completed manuscript or phonorecord plus $30.00 and a completed copyright form to the Copyright Office. When your story is published, you will want to make sure that a few dollars, in this case plus two published copies or phonorecords, go to the Copyright Office. For complete information, including a relatively simple application form, write the Register of Copyrights, Copyright Office, Library of Congress, Washington, D. C. 20559.

A New York Minute

Now back to selling the material that you've copyrighted. Again, an estimated twenty-million unpublished manuscripts appear annually in the United States, plus an exponentially larger amount elsewhere. It essentially is easier for the historic camel to go through the eye of a needle than for the remaining ninety-nine percent of authors of twenty-million or more manuscripts to receive other than form rejection slips for their efforts. Forty years ago a local publisher lugged to New York manuscripts for what would become Earl Tucker's three books, *How Not To Worry About The Love Life Of Spiders, Rambling Roses And Flying Bricks*, and *All The Nuts Aren't On Trees*. He made an appointment to meet the main agent (an Alabama native) at one of the largest literary agencies, but as he headed in the front door he espied the agent rushing out the back. That speeded his decision to publish them himself.

But first, while still in New York, he made an appointment with an official of the nation's largest independent book and magazine distribution agency, and traveled the length of the city to the appointment. An official had mentioned on the phone that his company might be interested in publishing the Earl Tucker books. But when he arrived about an hour later the official met him at his office doorway and pointed out that he had forgotten to mention that his company didn't publish books of newspaper columns. Some might call this an introduction to the "New York minute." The local publisher called Earl, and they decided to start small, and pray.

Yes, In The Final Analysis, Your Book's Best Friend Is Yourself

If your book is being produced by a publisher other than yourself, that publisher may take care of most or all of the preceding sales pitches. But certainly there is no guarantee. Unless your book is being heavily touted from the start as a bestseller, it can easily become lost among the nearly 50,000 books published annually in this country. Ultimately, in terms of your book's long-term health, you are its best doctor.

Famous Writers Who Were Self-Publishers

Dan Poynter's redoubtable *Self-Publishing Manual,* listed in this book's bibliography, names many famous self-publishers, such as James Fenimore Cooper, Washington Irving, Edgar Allan Poe, Percy Bysshe Shelley, Mark Twain, and Walt Whitman. Your name might read very well in this group.

Make It Easy To Order Your Published Book

The front of your book needs to include your publisher's address, phone number (perhaps an 800 number), and fax number if there is one. An order form in the back of your book will certainly increase its sales potential, and an order form can attract buyers for many years.

Make Sure That Your Publication Is Listed In Appropriate Reference Works

Members of the reading public, librarians, and booksellers use familiar reference volumes for ordering books. Most libraries have a reference department, and a reference librarian can help you select appropriate reference works. These include *Books In Print, Ulrich's International Perodicals Directory Cumulative Book Index,* H. W. Wilson catalogues, and Gale Research reference works. Alert them to your publication.

A News Release

Sometimes it helps to include a news release with your direct-mail advertising in addition to sending a copy to appropriate communication media. A news release should feature a sentence explaining why your book is newsworthy; samples of news releases can be found regularly in your newspaper.

Direct-Mail Advertising

In direct-mail advertising, a cover letter enclosing an advertising flyer with an order form on one side can be most effective. Of course a return envelope helps, and a stamped return envelope helps more. Many companies rent direct-mail lists. Publications that give the names and addresses of those that rent lists include *Literary Market Place* in many local libraries. Probably the market should first be tested with only a hundred or so mailouts. A 2 percent response is generally considered favorable enough to test a larger market.

See If A Distributor Will Handle Your Book

Twenty years ago, only large publishers had an adequate sales force to travel the countryside selling an author's books to bookstores and libraries. But then a wonderful new phenomenon emerged, namely independent distributors who handle titles from many publishers. Therefore, obtain names of a half dozen or so of these distributors to see which ones might help distribute your book. Many of them advertise in *Publishers Weekly*, for example, and your local bookseller or librarian should be able to help with additional identification.

Locate Books In Your Field Of Interest And Look At Their Bibliographies Listings

After checking in bibliographies, write to authors informing them about your book in their field. See if, for starters, they'll include it in their future bibliographies.

Two Helpful Newsletters For Smaller Publishers

Smaller publishers would be wise to belong to the Publishers Marketing Association (PMA) and The International Association Of Independent Publishers (called COSMEP, strangely enough). *Literary Market Place,* for example, contains association addresses, or your librarian can verify their current numbers. Included among intrinsic advantages in associating with kindred spirits, expect to find the newsletter of these two organizations especially helpful.

Things To Look For When Selecting A Distributor For Your Book

Does the distributor buy on consignment or buy outright, and at what price? Does the distributor have its own sales force or does it rely on phone calls and catalogues? How many accounts does the distributor have and over what territory? Does it handle direct mail sales and sales to non-book outlets? Which markets do you want the distributor to handle, and which do you wish to reserve for yourself?

Try To Sell To Bookstores And Bookstore Chains On A Nonreturnable Basis

Even if you give more (perhaps quite a bit more) than 50 percent discount, try to get your money up front or be prepared for frustration at best and loss of copies at worst. Most booksellers, as with other entrepreneurs, have a pecking order in terms of paying off invoices, and often the larger the publisher the greater the peck. Nonreturnable books sales up front can obviously help quiet your bill collectors.

Audio Books

Sales of more than 10,000 copies of audio books aren't unusual, so this is a definite market to consider for your book.

Consider Republishing An Out-Of-Print Or Struggling Book

To help your book gain attention, you might want to consider publishing a small run of a book in the same field to help add some clout. It could cost a few hundred or a few thousand dollars, but it could prove at least as interesting as a Caribbean cruise. Granted, this is a long-shot approach, but still on the range, so it's still our territory.

MARKETING ON THE INTERNET

A better title for this section could be, perhaps, HOW NOT TO MARKET ON THE INTERNET, since only a small percentage of us will end up marketing successfully on the Net. We read or hear rave success stories about companies such as Amazon books, a store that started small and grew to be a Net giant, or the firm in Pennsylvania selling chocolates. But we don't hear enough about the hundreds of thousands of unsuccessful vendors. Those luckless individuals thought they had built a better mousetrap and expected the world to beat a path to their door. Instead, the door remains closed. Firms promise to get anyone listed at or near the top if we pay enough. Such offers often begin as freebies but end as sales pitches.

But perhaps we construct our own Web site or pay an expert a hundred dollars or more to construct one for us. Surely we're in business at last. We tell our friends and they'll look and chances are they'll compliment our effort. But what about those hundreds of millions on the Internet who don't look us up and never will? Certainly a closed-door idea isn't what we envisioned when we started this thing.

Well, the preceding is the bad news. The good news is that at least a few of us will make it with customers indeed beating paths to our door. As to location of this path, the following six steps will at least point us in the right direction.

1. Try to select a business idea for our site on the Web that differs from one already in business in the real world. Or at least select one that can make special use of the Net's capabilities. If practical, let's think of a business that's unique. We can hardly overemphasize the importance of professional artistic design for our site on the Web.

2. We can set aside at least a couple hundred dollars to find a maker for our Website. (Of course, if we know how, we can pay ourselves). If we're lucky, we'll find an individual or firm (or they'll find us) who will take this money and make us an excellent Web site featuring what we have to offer. Probably our site should have the ability to display graphics as well as text that will include one or more links to something else on another page. (This linking of two or more items is a feature of hyper text language markup, or HTML on the Web.) If we don't know of a Web site maker, we can look at some sites on the Web, select one that we like, and then ask the owner of that Web site to identify who created it. There is no guarantee that the maker will treat us similarly, but at least we're not starting from scratch.

Instead of coming up with a single separate site, some businesses offer their pages through Internet access providers that cluster groups of business at one site. These so-called "cybermalls," or clustered storefronts, offer a very easy opportunity for a business to present its site. The malls normally provide services such as aid in developing pages, online order taking, and statistics concerning visitors to the page. The number of Web sites, including cybermalls, is predicted to continue growing very rapidly, their number now more than doubling in size every three months.

No matter who creates or maintains our Web site, we should make sure that it conforms to the traditional Internet "sharing philosophy." Some businesses offer links to related sites; others offer free copies of software, prizes, or new information. This is sometimes called the "gift economy" or the "giving back to the Net tradition." The Internet is built on the principle of being a good Net citizen. Such an adherence can help keep our Web-site marketing approach more in focus. This philosophy of giving back--the gift tradition--is unusually strong. Any business promoting its Web site would be very wise to heed such philosophy.

A well-constructed Web site is able to track the number of visitors to the site and the number of times the site has been addressed or hit. This logging of site activity can include how frequently the site has been visited, which pages were accessed the most often, and the e-mail addresses of the persons visiting the site.

3. Let's remember the old saying: If we're doing something someone else could do, they should have our job and we theirs. So let's have others prepare and maintain our Web site, unless we know how ourselves, while we concentrate on making our business a success. Let Ma Bell work for us with a toll free number and have the credit carders help us also. We don't have to do it all ourselves.

4. Let's evaluate our competition. We can get reactions from customers, or potential customers, either through e-mail or our toll-free phone.

5. We should be prepared to allocate a good percentage of our operating costs to marketing. To quote another, it takes money to make money.

6. Finally, let's be persistent in our sales approaches. We should try to tough it out for, let's say, at least a year. In the real world, five out of six new businesses don't make it through that first year. We can

certainly give a year to boundless possibilities with this new horizon called Internet.

Bread Upon The Water

Today in the dark clouds of cyberspace, silver linings are brighter. True, many clouds indeed are dark with so-called .coms going bankrupt almost faster than the referee can blow his whistle. A typical .com downsizing occurred today as technological giant Lucent announced downsizing a fresh 5,000 employees to the dark side.

Yet, in the preceding six steps one in particular is more than just shining. This step is "sharing." The Internet began with the goal of communication among mankind. The art of sharing information, for example. The more people help each other the clearer the space.

To make friends and otherwise influence people in Cyberspace, offer as much of yourself as you can. Free! People at the south pole wonder about Antartica's cold. If you know, tell them. Sooner or later, other things equal, you will get your just reward.

AN INTRODUCTION TO BIBLIOGRAPHY

One of the greatest rewards of a writer's life is that he can read all the books he wants without feeling guilty. This elusive guilt happened last night during a search for books to complete this book's bibliography. Found was a textbook used almost a half-century ago in a creative writing course at the University of Miami in Florida. Typically this class met outside the classroom in the shade of coconut palms, repeated now.

But let's return to the textbook assigned the Hurricanes by the University of Miami writing instructor. In a chapter entitled "Essentials Of The Short Story," one of approximately a hundred chapters, these points seemed overwhelming: "(1) The short story contains an interpretation of the writer's conception of life, either by direct statement or by implication; (2) A short story must produce a single effect upon the mind of the reader; (3) The short story must have a feeling of immediacy, and it appeals primarily to the emotions and only secondarily to the intellect; (4) The short story contains deliberately selected details and incidents, which may leave gaps and questions in the writer's mind."

It was precisely during the classroom discussion of point (4) that a coconut fell, almost leaving a gap in the mind of the lad from the north, and he's never relied heavily on this particular text since. But the reader with time and a roof may find it worthwhile, and it's included in the following bibliography for this book you're reading.

BIBLIOGRAPHY

American Book Trade Directory by R. R. Bowker Co., New York, updated periodically. <http://www.bowker.com>

American Library Directory by R. R. Bowker Co., New York, updated periodically. <http://www.bowker.com>

The Art of Writing for Publication by Kenneth Henson, Allyn and Bacon, Boston, MA, 1995. <http://www.abacon.com>

The Author's Handbook by Franklynn Peterson and Judi Kesselman-Turkel, Prentice Hall, Englewood Cliffs, NJ, 1982.

The Awful Truth About Publishing: Why They Always Reject Your Manuscript and What You Can Do About It by John Boswell, Warner Books, New York, 1986.

Becoming a Writer by Dorothy Brande, Boston, Houghton Mifflin, MA, 1981.

Beginning Writer's Answer Book edited by Kirk Polking and Rose Adkins, Writer's Digest Books, Cincinnati, OH, 1987. <http://www.writersdigest.com/>

Beyond Style: Mastering the Finer Points of Writing by Gary Provost, Writer's Digest Books, Cincinnati, OH, 1988. <http://www.writersdigest.com/>

Booklist by The American Library Association, Chicago, IL, monthly. <http://www.ala.org/booklist>

Book Review Digest by the H. W. Wilson Company, Bronx, NY, published monthly except February and July. < http://www.hwwilson.com >

Books In Print by R. R. Bowker Co., New York, NY, updated annually. < http://www.bowker.com >

The Chicago Manual of Style, For Authors, Editors, and Copywriters by the University of Chicago Press, Chicago, IL, updated periodically.
< http://www.press.uchicago.edu/News/manual_of_style.htm l>

Christian Writer's Market Guide by Sally Stuart, Harold Shaw Publishers, Wheaton, IL, 1997.

The Comedy Market: A Writer's Guide to Making Money Being Funny by Carmine DeSena, Berkley Publishing, New York, 1996.

Creative Nonfiction: Researching and Crafting Stories of Real Life by Philip Gerard, Story Press Books, Cincinnati, OH, 1996. < http://www.philipgerard.com >

Creating Short Fiction by Damon Knight, Writer=s Digest Books, Cincinnati, OH, 1985.
< http://www.writersdigest.com/ >

Creative Writing: For People Who Can't Not Write by Kathryn Lindskoog, Academia Books, Grand Rapids, Michigan, 1989.

Dartnell Direct Mail and Mail Order Handbook, edited by Richard S. Hodgson, Dartnell Corporation, Chicago, IL, 1980.

The Elements of Speechwriting and Public Speaking by Jeff

Scott Cook, Macmillan, New York, 1990.

The Elements of Style by William Strunk, Jr., and E. B. White, Macmillan, New York, 1979. < http://www.abacon.com >

Elements of the Writing Craft by Robert Olmstead, Story Press, Cincinnati, OH, 1997.

The Fiction Editor by Thomas McCormack, St. Martin=s Press, New York, 1988.

The Fine Art of Murder, edited by Ed Gorman, et. al., Carroll and Graf Publishers, New York, 1993.

The First Five Pages: a Writer's Guide to Staying out of the Rejection Pile by Noah Lukeman, Simon and Schuster, New York, 2000. < http://www.lukeman.com >

Th*e Forest for the Trees: an Editor's Advice to Writers* by Betsy Lerner, Riverhead Books, New York, 2000.

The Freelance Writer's Survival Guide: a Comprehensive Handbook for both New and Experienced Writer's by Robert Pelton and Jeanne Ridley, Betterway Publications, White Hall, VA, 1990.

Gale Directory of Publications and Broadcast Media, Gale Research, Inc., Detroit, MI, updated periodically. < http://www.gale.com >

Handbook for Freelance Writing by Michael Perry, NTC Business Books, Lincolnwood, IL, 1998.

How To Be a Great Communicator: in Person, on Paper, and on the Podium by Nido Qubein, J. Wiley, New York, 1997. < www.nidoqubein.com >

How To Get Happily Published by Judith Appelbaum, HarperCollins, New York, 1998. <http://www.harpercollins.com>

How To Publicize Your Way to Success: a Step-by-Step Guide by Bonnie Weiss, Catalyst Publications, San Francisco, CA, 1985.

How To Write a Book Proposal by Michael Larsen, Writer's Digest Books, Cincinnati, OH, 1985. <http://www.writersdigest.com/>

How To Write a Children=s Book and Get It Published by Barbara Seuling, Scribner, New York, 1991.

How To Write a Cookbook and Get it Published by Sara Pitzer, Writers's Digest Books, Cincinnati, OH, 1984. <http://www.writersdigest.com/>

How To Write a Manual by Elizabeth Slatkin, Ten Speed Press, Berkeley, CA, 1991.

How To Write a Memoir [sound recording] by William Zinsser, HarperCollins, New York, 1999.

How To Write a Mystery by Larry Beinhart, Ballantine Books, New York, 1996. <http://www.randomhouse.com>

How To Write and Publish a Classic Cookbook by Rolfe Hays and Associates, New American Library, 1986.

How To Write and Publish Your Family Book by Genealogy Publishing Service, Franklin, NC, 1995.

How To Write (and Sell) a Christian novel: Proven and Practical Advice from a Best-selling Author by Gilbert Morris,

Vine Books, Ann Arbor, Michigan, 1994.

How To Write and Sell Your First Nonfiction Book by Oscar Collier and Frances Leighton, St. Martin's Press, New York, 1990.

How To Write and Sell Your Personal Experiences by Lois Duncan, Writer's Digest Books, Cincinnati, OH, 1979.
< http://www.writersdigest.com/ >

How To Write Articles That Sell by L. Perry Wilbur and Jon Samsel, Allworth Press, New York, 1999.

How To Write Books that Sell by L. Perry Wilbur and Jon Samsel, Allworth Press, New York, 1998.

How To Write Fast (While Writing Well) by David Fryxell Writer's Digest Books, Cincinnati, OH, 1992.
< http://www.writersdigest.com/ >

How To Write Horror Fiction by William Nolan, Writer's Digest Books, Cincinnati, OH, 1990.
< http://www.writersdigest.com/ >

How To Write Like an Expert About Anything by Hank Nuwer, Writer's Digest Books, Cincinnati, OH, 1995.
< http://www.writersdigest.com/ >

How To Write Mysteries by Shannon O'Cork, Writer's Digest Books, Cincinnati, OH, 1989.
< http://www.writersdigest.com/ >

How To Write Poetry by Paul Janeczko, Scholastic Reference, New York, 1999.

How to Write Romances by Phyllis Taylor Pianka, Writer's

Digest Books, Cincinnati, OH, 1988.
<http://www.writerscomputer.com/store/info/how_to_write_
romances.htm>

How To Write Western Novels by Matt Braun, Writer's Digest
Books, Cincinnati, OH, 1988.
<http://www.mattbraun.com/home.htm>

How To Write What You Want and Sell What You Write by
Skip Press/Career Press, Franklin Lakes, NJ, 1995.

International Literary Market Place by R. R. Bowker, New
York, updated periodically. <http://www.bowker.com>

Literary Market Place by R. R. Bowker Co., New York,
updated annually. <http://www.literarymarketplace.com/>

Market Guide for Young Writer's by Kathy Henderson, Talman
Co., New York, 1988.

MLA Style Manual and Guide to Scholarly Publishing by
Joseph Gibaldi, Modern Language Association of America,
New York, 1998. <http://mla.org>

On Writing Well: An Informal Guide to Writing Non-fiction,
Harper Perennial, New York, 1990.

1001 Ways To Market Your Books-For Publishers and Authors
by John Kremer, Open Horizons, Fairfield, IA, updated
periodically. <http://www.bookmarket.com>

The Poet's Handbook by Judson Jerome, Writer's Digest
Books, Cincinnati, OH, 1980.
<http://www.writerscomputer.com/store/info/poets_hanbook
.htm>

The Poet's Marketplace: the Definitive Sourcebook on Where to Get Your Poems Published by Joseph Kelly, Running Press, Philadelphia, PA, 1984.

Publicity for Books and Authors: A Do-It-Yourself Handbook For Small Publishing Firms and Enterprising Authors by Peggy Glenn, Aames-Allen Publishing, Huntington Beach, CA, 1985.

Publishers Trade List Annual by R. R. Bowker Co., New York, updated annually, other titles: Subject Guide to Books In Print; Books In Print.
< http://www.bowker.com/bowkerweb/ >

Publishers Weekly by R. R. Bowker Co., New York, published weekly.   < http://www.publishersweekly.com/ >

The Random House Guide to Good Writing by Mitchell Ivers, Random House, New York, 1991.

Religious Writers Marketplace by William H. Gentz, Running Press, Philadelphia, PA, 1989.

The Rights of Authors, Artists, and Other Creative People by Jerry Simon Chasen and Kenneth P. Norwick, Southern Illinois University Press, Carbondale, IL, 1992.

The Right to Write: an Invitation and Initiation into the Writing Life by Julia Cameron, Putnam, New York, 1998.
< www.sun-angel.com >

School Library Journal, R. R. Bowker Co., New York, NY, published monthly.   < http://www.slj.com/ >

The Self-Publishing Manual: How To Write, Print & Sell Your Own Book by Dan Poynter, Para Publishing, Santa Barbara, CA, 2000, updated periodically.

< http://www.parapublishing.com

Starting from Scratch: a Different Kind of Writer's Manual by Rita Mae Brown, Bantam Books, New York, 1988.

Subject Guide to Books in Print and Forthcoming Books by R.R. Bowker Co., New Providence, NJ, updated periodically. < http://www.bowker.com >

Tools of the Writer's Trade: Writers Tell all About the Equipment and Services They Find the Best/ the American Society of Journalists and Authors Edited by Dodi Schultz, HarperCollins, New York, 1990.

The 29 Most Common Writing Mistakes and How to Avoid Them by Judy Delton, Writer's Digest Books, Cincinnati, OH, 1985. < http://www.writersdigest.com/ >

Write and Sell Your Free-Lance Article by Linda Allen, The Writer, Boston, MA, 1991.

The Writer Got Screwed (But Didn't Have To): A Guide to the Legal and Business Practices of Writing for the Entertainment Industry by Brooke Wharton, HarperCollins Publishers, New York, 1996.

The Writer's Advisor by Leland Alkire, JR. and Cheryl Westerman, Gale Research Co, Detroit, Michigan, 1985.

A Writer's America: Landscape in Literature by Alfred Kazin, A.A. Knopf, New York, 1988.

The Writer's Art by James J. Kilpatrick, Andrews McMeel Publishing, Kansas City, KS, 1985.

The Writer's Book of Checklists: the Quick Reference Guide to

Essential Information Every Writer Needs by Scott Edelstein, Writer's Digest Books, Cincinnati, OH, 1990.
< http://www.writersdigest.com/ >

Writer's Digest by Writer's Digest, Cincinnati, OH, published monthly.   < http://www.writersdigest.com/ >

The Writer's Digest Guide to Good Writing edited by Thomas Clark, Writer's Digest Books, Cincinnati, OH, 1994.
< http://www.writersdigest.com/ >

Writer's Digest Handbook of Making Money Freelance Writing edited by Amanda Boyd, Writer's Digest Books, Cincinnati, OH, 1997. < http://www.writersdigest.com/ >

The Writer's Digest Handbook of Novel Writing edited by Tom Clark, Writer's Digest Books, Cincinnati, OH, 1992.
< http://www.writersdigest.com/ >

The Writer's Essential Desk Reference edited by Glenda Tennant Neff, Writer's Digest Books, Cincinnati, OH, 1991.
< http://www.writersdigest.com/ >

Writer's Guide to Book Editors, Publishers, and Literary Agents 2001-2002: Who They Are! What They Want! And How To Win Them Over! by Jeff Herman, Prima Publishing, Rocklin, CA, 2000, updated periodically.
< http://www.primalifestyles.com/books/book/3786 >

The Writer's Guide to Creating a Science Fiction Universe by George Ochoa and Jeffrey Osier, Writer's Digest Books, Cincinnati, OH, 1993. < http://www.writersdigest.com/ >

The Writer's Guide to the Internet by Dawn Groves, Beedle and Associates, Wilsonville, OR, 1996.

The Writer's Handbook edited by Udia G. Olsen, The Writer, Inc., Boston, MA, updated annually.

Writer's Inc: a Guide to Writing, Thinking, and Learning by Patrick Sebranek, Verne Meyer, Dave Kemper, Write Source Pub. House, Burlington, Wis., 1990.

The Writer's Legal Companion by Brad Bunnin and Peter Beren, Addison-Wesley Publishing Company, Reading, MA, 1994.

The Writer's Legal Guide by Tad Crawford and Tony Lyons, Allworth Press, New York, 1996.
< http://www.allworth.com/catalog/WR114.htm >

The Writer's Market Companion by Joe Feiertag, Mary Cupito, and the editors of Writer's Market, Writer's Digest Books, Cincinnati, OH, 2000. < http://www.writersdigest.com/ >

Writer's Market: Where And How To Sell What You Write by Writer's Digest Books, Cincinnati, OH, updated annually. < http://www.writersdigest.com/ >

Writing, A to Z: the Terms, Procedures, and Facts of the Writing Business Defined, Explained, and Put Within Reach edited by Kirk Polking, Joan Bloss, and Colleen Cannon, Writer's Digest Books, Cincinnati, OH, 1990. < http://www.writersdigest.com/ >

Writing 101 by Claudia Sorsby, St. Martin's Press, New York, 1996.

Writing Articles From the Heart: How to Write and Sell Your Life Experiences by Marjorie Holmes, Writer's Digest Books, Cincinnati, OH, 1993. < http://www.writersdigest.com/ >

Writing for Children and Teenagers by Lee Wyndham, Writer's Digest Books, Cincinnati, OH, 1997. < http://www.writersdigest.com/ >

Writing Crime Fiction by H.R.F. Keating, St. Martins Press, New York, 1987.

Writing Down the Bones: Freeing the Writer Within by Natalie Goldberg, Random House, Boston, MA, 1986.

Writing for Engineering and Science by Tyler Gregory Hicks, McGraw Hill, New York, 1961.

Writing for Money by Loriann Oberlin, Writer's Digest Books, Cincinnati, OH, 1994. < http://www.writersdigest.com/ >

Writing Mysteries: A Handbook edited by Sue Grafton, Writer's Digest Books, Cincinnati, OH, 1992. < http://www.writersdigest.com/ >

Writing Nonfiction that Sells by Sam Sinclair Baker, Writer's Digest Books, Cincinnati, OH, 1986. < http://www.writersdigest.com/ >

Writing Poetry: Where Poems Come From and How to Write Them by David Kerby, The Writer Inc., Boston, MA, 1997. < http://www.channel1.com/the writer/ >

Writing Romances: A Handbook edited by Rita Gallagher and Rita Clay Estrada, Writer's Digest Books, Cincinnati, OH, 1997. < http://www.writersdigest.com/ >

Writing and Selling Magazine Articles by Eva Shaw, Paragon House, New York, 1992.

Your Autobiography: More Than 300 Questions to Help You

Write Your Personal History by Ray Mungo, Maxwell Macmillan International, New York, 1994.

GLOSSARY

A

AAP: Association of American Publishers

ABA: American Booksellers Association

ABI: Advance Book Information. Major points about future titles

ALA: American Library Association

B

back list: Publisher's previously published books still in print and available, though not part of the publisher's "active list."

bar code: A bar, usually on a book's back cover, that includes price.

bibliography: That part of a publication that lists books or other information used by the author in his work, or that the author recommends.

bleed: Ink goes all the way to the paper's edge.

blueline: final proof before printing.

blurb: Promotional material praising an author or publication.

boards: Camera-ready copy ready for the printer.

bullet: A large black dot often used to highlight an item in a list.

C

camera-ready: Copy ready for camera and press.
copy

CIS: Coated One Side. Printers use this to declare that stock is smooth on one side only.

caption: Words explaining a picture or illustration.

case binding: Hardcover binding, as contrasted with softcover binding.

clip art: A collection of illustrations or pictures used for embellishing text.

clipping service: A firm that clips items of interest to a customer.

color separation: Different color lenses separate red, blue, and yellow--the three primary colors--and black, in color illustrations and photographs.

co-op advertising: Typically a publisher and bookstore share the cost of an ad, the publisher paying the larger amount.

co-op publishing: More than one person, or firms, join in publishing.

copy editing: Editing a manuscript, primarily for grammar, punctuation, and spelling.

copyright: The Copyright Office, Library Of Congress, Washington 25 D. C., has clear and simple instructions for copyrighting. Check the index for more information.

Crane: Prepublication galley, named for the printer widely known for these galleys.

crop marks: Marks showing desired print boundaries of photographs or illustrations.

D

distributor: A firm that warehouses, markets, and distributes publications for you.

dump: A display for books, usually temporary, made of cardboard.

dust jacket: The paper around a publication, originally to keep dust off it.

E

ebook: An electronic book. Readers read on monitors or hear words audibly that are printed electronically rather than with ink on paper.

ergonomics: A study of how workers react to their work environment. In ergonomics we design objects in the work place, such as keyboards and chairs, in a manner that provides safety and comfort for workers.

epilogue: A concluding section that rounds out a literary work.

F

fair use: The permissible legal use of a limited amount of copyrighted material without the owner's permission.

fax: While a fax usually is sent and received with a stand-alone fax machine, a fax also can be sent to or from a computer using fax computer instructions and a modem. But a problem here is that the receiving computer must be turned on at the time--a costly and inconvenient feature.

flat: A printing term describing the collection of negatives on a paper sheet prior to plate-making.

flush: To be even, as in "flush right."

foreword: Introductory remarks about the book or the author.

front matter: All the material in a publication before the text.

frontispiece: An illustration opposite the title page.

G

galley: A galley is a proof after something is printed. Publishers often send it in book form to major book reviewers.

gutter: The space between sections of type including the space between margins of facing pages.

H

hardcopy: Something printed. For instance, the soft paper that comes from a printer is hard copy.

hardcover: A book bound with boards or material of similar strength.

I

ISBN: International Standard Book Number is a number that identifies the edition, binding, and publisher of a book. Issued by the R. R. Bowker Company, it is an important identification number throughout the book's life.

J

jobber: Buys books for resale to stores, libraries, and other customers.

justification: Right and left margins of text are even.

K

kerning: Changing space between letters. A kern is part of a typeset letter that projects beyond its sides.

L

laser printer: The top of the line printer for PCs. This printer uses a laser beam to create the image on paper.

leading: The amount of vertical spacing, measured in points, between lines of type.

library rate: A cheaper U. S. Postal rate for shipping publications to or from libraries and educational institutions.

list price: In publishing, the price on a publication's cover.

logo: An illustration that identifies its owner.

lowercase: Short letters, not capitals.

M

mass-market: Smaller (4 X 7), cheaper paperbacks. paperback

N

negative: The image of the original in the Traditional Printing process. The negatives are changed to positive prints.

O

overruns: Printing more than contracted for. Printers typically are granted overruns and underruns of 10% or less.

P

paperback: A softcover book.

PDF: Portable Document Format, produced by Adobe Acrobat, is a program now required by many printers to facilitate acceptance of manuscripts submitted as a file or files.

plagiarism: To steal and pass off the ideas and words of another as one's own.

PMS: The Pantone Matching System for selecting colors.

POD: Print On Demand, now feasible because of electronic printing.

ppi: Pages per inch. Used in determining the potential thickness of a publication.

preface: In the front of a publication, introductory remarks by the author.

PMA: Publishers Marketing Association, the nation's largest, helps members sell publications.

Q

quotes: Publishers obtain quotes from printers, typically several, concerning the cost and speed of printing jobs.

R

remaindering: The selling of excess publications after a title nears backlist status or discontinuance.

running heads: The title at the top of a page, normally either a chapter or publication title.

S

scanner: In printing, a device that scans material, such as text or photographs, and transmits the image into a printing machine. In more familiar form, a widely used example of scanning occurs when goods are scanned at store cash registers.

serif: Tails on a printed character make it easier to read say serif proponents.

signature: A publication folded into sections for printing purposes. Such sections often contain standard increments of 16 or 32 pages.

Smyth sewn: Pages are sewn together with thread in most hardbound books in contrast with glue used in softcovers.

Special Standard U. S. Postal Rates: Despite the title publishers may have trouble learning such rates. Here at Edorts several calls to the post office resulted in different rate quotations. So we're using the lowest rate given, and so far no mailing has been returned.

stet: From the Latin "To stand." Stet is a proofreading term requesting that the item be left as is.

subsidy press: A publisher who charges the author to publish his work. Book reviewers in particular seem critical of this so-called Vanity Publishing.

T

trim marks: Marks used to show boundaries of material to be printed.

U

underrun: A printer prints less than the quantity ordered. See overrun.

V

vanity press or vanity publisher: author pays for more than the printing.

W

web press: A large press, printing on rolls rather than sheets.

working title: In a publishing project a title used until the permanent title is named.

INDEX

COMPUTERS

IN

PLAIN

ENGLISH

Edorts' most recent technological book, *Computers In Plain English,* is another Akens publication. One of Akens' favorite topics is that clarity of expression is a hallmark of good writing. Among the computer book's conclusions, literary newcomers to computers must not only learn computers technically they must walk a confusing semantical swinging bridge.

Basic material for his books come, Akens says, from his studies as a creative writing student on more than a half-dozen college campuses, as well as his experience heading printing and publishing firms. His literary interests reflect this varied professional background.

Computers In Plain English as well as *How To Write And Get It Published* are premier among Akens' many publications.

EDORTS

PUBLISHING

COMPANY

EASY ORDER NOW

Telephone: Toll free. 1 800 655 7240

Email: abookcoup@aol.com

Fax: 256 881 4060

Please send the following books: 1. COMPUTERS IN PLAIN ENGLISH $12.95 plus $3.00 mailing and handling; or 2. HOW TO WRITE AND GET IT PUBLISHED $12.95 plus $3.00 mailing and handling. I understand that I may return either or both for a prompt and complete refund.

MY NAME IS

Name_____

Address_____

City_____

Telephone_____

Email_____

Payment: 1. Check 2. Master Card 3. Visa

Card Number_____

Expiration Date_____

Name on card_____

Name On Card_____

EDORTS

PUBLISHING

COMPANY

EASY ORDER NOW

Telephone: Toll free. 1 800 655 7240

Email: abookcoup@aol.com

Fax: 256 881 4060

Please send the following books: 1. COMPUTERS IN PLAIN ENGLISH $12.95 plus $3.00 mailing and handling; or 2. HOW TO WRITE AND GET IT PUBLISHED $12.95 plus $3.00 mailing and handling. I understand that I may return either or both for a prompt and complete refund.

MY NAME IS

Name_____

Address_____

City_____

Telephone_____

Email_____

Payment: 1. Check 2. Master Card 3. Visa

Card Number_____

Expiration Date_____

Name on card_____

Name On Card_____